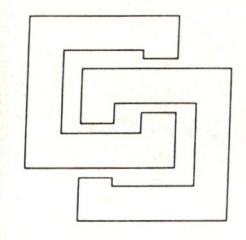

The Changing Face of Work

European Foundation
for the Improvement of Living and Working Conditions

Loughlinstown House, Shankill, Co. Dublin, Ireland. Tel: (01) 826888 Telex: 30726 EURF EI Fax: 826456

This publication is available in French as a
Working Paper. Reference No. EF/WP/88/07/FR

Cataloguing data can be found at the end of this publication.

Luxembourg: Office for Official Publications of the European Communities, 1988

ISBN 92-825-8595-6

Catalogue number: SY-52-88-590-EN-C

© Copyright: THE EUROPEAN FOUNDATION FOR THE IMPROVEMENT OF LIVING AND WORKING CONDITIONS, 1988. For rights of translation or reproduction, applications should be made to the Director, European Foundation for the Improvement of Living and Working Conditions, Loughlinstown House, Shankill, County Dublin, Ireland.

Printed in Ireland

The European Foundation for the Improvement of Living and Working Conditions

THE CHANGING FACE OF WORK:
Researching & debating the issues

by

Françoise PIOTET

Paris

October 1987

Contract No: 86/4-4030-22

Preface

Many of the forces which are transforming the organization of industry and services are also bringing about a redefinition of work. For many people "work" no longer holds its traditional meaning of remunerated, full-time, on-site employment. Shiftwork patterns are changing with evolving social demands and technological innovations. New forms of work and activity are emerging to overcome "rigidities" in the labour market. The introduction of automated systems is causing manual labour to be increasingly replaced by monitoring, control and maintenance functions.

The Foundation has been examining different aspects of these issues for some time now. In 1985 it launched a research programme on New Forms of Work and Activity. Related to this, the reorganization of work has featured for many years in the Foundation's work programme on the impact of introducting new technology.

Increased flexibility in the labour market has facilitated the development of certain atypical work situations which the Foundation is studying in this programme. These new ways of working include: different types of contracts, such as part-time or temporary work; different arrangements of working time, such as permanent week-end work, on-call work, 12-hour shifts; and certain work forms featuring different locations, such as isolated work, home work, and telework.

In order to obtain a state of the art picture the Foundation commissioned Professor Françoise Piotet to review and analyse current research material, particularly of a quantitative nature. The ensuing report which is presented in this volume indicates that there is a real interest in flexibility and a move away from salary-related issues as the sole object of collective bargaining, particularly in countries with relatively high income levels. It became clear that interest in this area is not based on futuristic ideas but on an emerging new reality. Gaps in research are also identified. Most existing work was mainly national research, and few international comparative surveys on new forms of work had as yet been made.

This work is an invaluable contribution to the development of the Foundation's programme on New Forms of Work and Activity. It offers important insight into the problem from a research design point of view and can therefore provide guidance to the further development of the Foundation's activities in this field.

Eberhard Köhler
Research Manager

Dublin
March 1988

Page

Contents

Introduction   1

Part 1: Analyses

I.   Description of new forms of work   5

     a) The battle of the figures   5
        . as seen statically
        . as seen dynamically

     b) The law and its application   24

     c) Flexibility in practice   30

II. Predictions   36

     a) From the boundaries of description...   36

     b) ... to the limits of prediction   46

Part 2: Opinions   53

I.   Surveys among workers   56

     a) Money rather than time   57

     b) Flexibility rather than rigidity   62

     c) Solidarity, despite everything   65

     d) But "vive la différence"   67

II.	The opinions of employers	69
1.	Manufacturing industry	69
	a) Background	69
	. Fairly pessimistic outlook	
	. Too many unskilled workers, too few skilled workers	
	b) Obstacles to recruitment: the reasons given	73
	c) Relaxation of constraints... without a consensus	77
	d) Flexible working-time arrangements	86
	e) ... and job-sharing	92
2.	Wholesale and retail trade	94
	a) Background: wait and see	94
	b) Lower wages for new starters rather than reduced working hours	95
	c) Ultimately satisfactory opening hours... which could be completely deregulated	99
	d) And, as in manufacturing industry, why not job-sharing?	99
	e) What conclusions can we draw from this rather hazy picture?	100
III.	In conclusion: prescriptions...	107
Annexes		111

Introduction

Research, studies, debates, seminars and conferences on new forms of work have been so increasingly prolific in Europe and the USA over the past decade that we have reached the point where it would be quite unrealistic to hold any hope of producing an exhaustive account of the ideas and controversies raised by the subject. Such a task would undoubtedly prove difficult merely at national level and would therefore be nigh on impossible if we were to attempt to extend coverage to all the Member States of the European Community.

Hence, although our approach may be somewhat unorthodox in terms of the generally accepted method of presenting a study report, we feel that it is essential to begin by stating what our report is not.

Firstly, as we have already intimated, and even though it could be of very considerable value, our intention is not to provide a comprehensive, annotated list of all the publications dealing with new forms of work and activity in the Community countries; this task has in any case already been tackled, at least in part, at both national and Community level (Sarfati and Kobrin, 1987).

Neither are we concerned with "researching the research", which would consist in analysing the relevance of the hypotheses put forward by the publications under examination or the validity of the results obtained. Nor, even though it would be an especially fruitful and informative exercise, is this a report that singles out the major preoccupations of current research, an approach which could result in limiting our investigations of current changes to merely the lines of inquiry actually pursued by the researchers.

Our aim is in fact, having consulted a very large number of documents and having listened to and questioned many researchers, to discover to what extent research projects answer the questions being raised by employers, trade unions and governments, since the primary objective of the Foundation's work is to aid the decision-makers.

The purpose and chosen method underlying our report are therefore interdependent. We shall not only make no attempt to be exhaustive, but shall also select our references, restricting ourselves as far as possible to European studies, ie works conceived as comparative studies right from the start.

Lastly, in referring to "new forms of work" we shall be using the definition approved by participants at the Brussels Colloquium, the Proceedings of which have been published by the Foundation, although we are obviously aware that the topic evokes the undoubtedly wider and still more uncertain theme of "flexibility".

The first part of this report deals with works and studies centring mainly on behaviour and its analysis. Behaviour here is interpreted in a very wide sense as it covers both the behaviour of individuals and that of firms, the public authorities and the two sides of industry, ie of the entire economy. This first part of the report has been divided into two chapters entitled "Description" & "Prediction" respectively.

Although the alliteration may have a pleasant ring, these headings were chosen not for stylistic effect but because they seemed particularly evocative of the problems raised in the debates on new forms of work.

The first problem is very much one of description. Apart from the fact that we need to know what we are talking about and to define the scope of these new forms of work and activity, it is also essential to have a very concrete conception of them. What sort of numbers are involved? Who are the employees being affected? In which firms (as regards both size and sector of activity)? What legal and contractual frameworks govern these new forms of work and activity? And what actual practices follow in their wake?

The second question covers many _predictive_ aspects, because although these new forms of work do exist, many of them have been in use for too little time (or have been studied and identified too recently) for their full impact to have been felt. They are therefore the subject of a very large number of fundamental theoretical publications both at macroeconomic level, in the interpretation of trends in the general system of labour, and at macrosocial level, in assessing the impact of changes in the world of work on the life of individuals, which cannot fail to raise problems regarding regulation and solidarity at the same time.

A third approach, which will serve as a conclusion, gathers together publications which are based mainly on _prescription_. In response to the difficulties faced by firms and also with a view to tackling very high unemployment, the public authorities, the two sides of industry and the experts have recommended certain measures, some of which are related to our topic here. These measures may have been criticized by researchers concerned with anticipating the consequences within the framework of a predictive approach and may therefore also be mentioned in the previous section; this simply shows that all classifications are somewhat arbitrary and bound to include some repetition and overlapping.

Having reviewed some of the main European research relating to new forms of work "in the flesh", it seemed sensible to look at data on the opinions of the people most affected: employees and employers. We already have some idea of their opinions as voiced by their representatives in the trade unions and employers' associations and mentioned in the first part of the report. The aim in the second part is rather to give an account of European surveys on new forms of work and activity, given that a multitude of national surveys on the subject have been conducted but that the results are often highly contradictory and do not allow any comparison between countries.

Finally, this second part of the report can be seen as an important area for thought. Opinions are not necessarily reflected in behaviour: employers may be fully convinced that they would recruit staff if the administrative constraints on dismissal were lifted, but do not necessarily put their words into action if the constraints are indeed lifted, as we have seen in France. In the same way, employees may feel very inclined to accept certain alterations in working time yet refuse them when they are actually offered. This means that opinions must be taken for what they are and nothing more. Opinions in fact indicate the psychological obstacles that may need to be surmounted if certain changes are introduced or, on the contrary, if they are opposed. Yet opinion does exist and consideration of it is part of the art of government, even if this art also sometimes consists of having the courage to go against opinion.

Part 1: Analyses

I. Description of new forms of work

The first paradox to become apparent is that so many research projects relate to this subject and yet so few bother to define "new forms of work" and even fewer to measure their extent.

a) The battle of the figures

The first comment often made (Foundation, 1986) is that there are in fact extremely few very noteworthy innovations in employment and that the majority of these new forms of work are actually very old. On the other hand, it is often pointed out that the distinguishing feature of the phenomenon is its sudden growth. It is undoubtedly true that these forms of work, whether part-time or temporary jobs, fixed-term contracts or even home working, are not new, yet they are now experiencing a popularity unequalled in industrial history.

... as seen statically

There is a very lively debate over this apparently simple analysis. People in favour of flexibility claim that, in absolute terms, the number of jobs involved is small or very small, with the exception perhaps of part-time work.

For all that, the debate over figures is one which at national level, and all the more so at European level, rests on very shaky foundations: in a number of areas we have either no data at all or very imprecise data (Eurostat, 1987) and it is extremely difficult to compare data which are not necessarily comparable because the regulations or definitions vary from country to country.

The latest OECD publication on Employment Trends is interesting in this respect. We shall first look at the new form of work which is the most significant in terms of volume: part-time working.

Extent and composition of part-time working, 1979-86

| | \multicolumn{9}{c|}{Part-time working as a proportion of} | \multicolumn{3}{c|}{Women's share} |
| | total employment ||| male employment ||| female employment ||| of part-time working |||
	1979	1983	1986	1979	1983	1986	1979	1983	1986	1979	1983	1986
Belgium	6.0	8.1	8.6	1.0	2.0	1.9	16.5	19.7	21.1	89.3	84.0	86.1
Denmark	22.7	23.7	23.8	5.2	6.6	8.4	46.3	44.7	43.9	86.9	84.7	80.9
France	8.2	9.7	11.7	2.5	2.6	3.5	17.0	20.1	23.1	82.0	84.6	83.0
Germany	11.2	12.6	12.3	1.5	1.7	2.1	27.6	30.0	28.4	91.6	91.9	89.8
Greece		6.5			3.7			12.1			61.2	
Ireland	5.1	6.7	6.5	2.1	2.7	2.4	13.1	15.7	15.5	71.2	72.0	74.3
Italy	5.3	4.6	5.3	3.0	2.4	3.0	10.6	9.4	10.1	61.4	64.8	61.6
Netherlands	11.1	22.0	24.0	2.8	7.8	8.7	31.7	50.5	54.2	82.5	76.2	76.1
UK	16.4	19.1	21.2	1.9	3.3	4.2	39.0	42.4	44.9	92.8	89.6	88.5
Luxembourg	5.8	6.7	7.3	1.0	1.0	2.6	17.1	18.8	16.3	64.5	70.7	70.0

Source: OECD, *Employment Trends*, September 1987

An analysis of these figures shows that, since 1979, the proportion of total employment accounted for by part-time working has increased in all the Community countries for which data are available, with the exception of Italy, where it plummeted in 1983 and then rose to its 1979 level again in 1986. The increase is particularly significant - even spectacular - in the Netherlands, where the proportion has risen from 11% to 24%, and to a lesser degree in the UK (16.4% to 21.2%).

France is gradually catching up with the Federal Republic of Germany, crossing the 10% mark between 1983 and 1986, while all the other countries are below, or even well below, that figure.

The second comment prompted by this table refers to the wide difference in practices in the various countries. Three countries are very heavy users of part-time work - Denmark, the UK and the

Netherlands, where it accounts for a quarter of total employment - while other Member States, such as Italy, Ireland and even Belgium, resort to it only sparingly.

The third important observation concerns the proportion of part-time working in relation to female employment. Some of the figures are startling: more than half (54.2%) of jobs held by women in the Netherlands are part-time. In other words, half of the female working population works only half-time. The situation is similar in Denmark and the UK (43.9% and 44.9%). In Germany, France and Belgium, the proportion is between 20% and 25% and it is, naturally, at its lowest in Italy.

The proportion of part-time working in relation to male employment obviously has nothing in common with the figures just quoted. The Netherlands has seen a strong increase in the proportion of part-time jobs for men, rising from 2.8% in 1979 to 8.7% in 1986, but this is in line with the general increase in part-time working in that country. It is interesting to note a trend reversal in Denmark: the proportion of male part-time jobs increased from 5.2% to 8.4% while the proportion of part-time jobs for women, although still very high, fell over the same period.
(See table on following page)

Part-time working as a proportion of total employment by sector, 1983 and 1985[a]

	All sectors	Agriculture, forestry, fisheries & hunting	Energy & water	Mining industries & chemical products	Iron & steel & engineering industries	Other manufacturing industries
Belgium						
1983	8.1	6.2	1.0	1.9	1.9	3.8
1985	8.6	7.2	1.2	1.7	1.6	4.3
France						
1983	9.7	16.5	3.5	2.1	2.2	5.6
1985	10.8	15.6	3.8	2.6	1.2	5.8
Ireland						
1983	6.7	9.4	1.8	1.8	2.5	3.6
1985	6.5	7.9	1.2	1.3	1.6	2.9
Italy						
1983	4.6	13.3	1.2	1.1	1.2	3.6
1985	5.3	14.3	2.2	1.6	1.6	4.3
Luxembourg						
1983	6.7	15.9	0.0	1.2	2.0	4.7
1985	7.3	13.4	0.0	1.8	5.1	5.0
Netherlands[b]						
1983	22.0	17.7			6.5	
1985	24.0	17.6			10.3	
United Kingdom						
1983	19.1	14.9	3.3	5.6	5.0	12.2
1985	21.2	17.8	2.9	5.7	5.1	13.8

Part-time working as a proportion of total employment by sector, 1983 and 1985[a]

	Building & public works	Distribution trade	Transport & communications	Banking, insurance, property & services for firms	Other services	Public administration
Belgium						
1983	2.1	11.0	2.4	10.1	17.6	4.7
1985	2.7	11.2	2.8	10.0	17.4	7.4
France						
1983	3.9	10.6	5.4	9.2	17.5	10.2
1985	4.4	12.1	6.7	10.8	19.4	13.4
Ireland						
1983	2.6	10.2	4.0	4.0	10.8	2.7
1985	1.8	9.7	4.3	4.7	12.5	2.5
Italy						
1983	2.7	4.2	1.4	2.9	6.7	0.9
1985	3.5	5.1	1.6	3.3	7.7	1.7
Luxembourg						
1983	1.5	7.3	3.2	5.1	13.2	7.4
1985	4.5	8.6	4.3	5.7	12.5	7.0
Netherlands[b]						
1983	5.8	23.3	12.8	16.8	40.9	33.8
1985	6.6	24.9	12.1	19.8	45.5	33.7
United Kingdom						
1983	4.5	33.5	5.8	14.4	36.3	8.9
1985	6.3	35.5	6.5	15.3	38.8	10.3

a. The figures cover everyone in employment, with the exception of those for whom no classification was available by type of employment (part-time/full-time) or by sector.

b. The figures for the Netherlands are based on the SBI system for the classification of sectors of activity. They refer only to those employees whose working hours were specified (see note a. to Table 1.3). This means that the figures may be influenced by variations, both over time and between sectors, in the proportion of people in employment for whom working hours were indicated. These discrepancies were generally relatively slight, except for the transport and communications sector. In 1983, more than 20% of all employees in this sector were not classified according to their working hours, as against only 2% in 1985. Employment in this sector is however included under the column headed "All sectors".

Sources: The figures for the Netherlands were supplied by the Ministry for Social Affairs and Employment. The figures for the other countries were provided by Eurostat and are based on the results of national surveys on the labour force.

If we now look at part-time working as a proportion of total employment by sector of activity, it is immediately apparent that the proportion is highest in the service sector. Yet here again, there are significant differences between countries: part-time working represents 5% of total employment in the distribution trade in Italy, as against 33.5% in the UK.

The column headed "Other services" includes social and public services, which employ the highest number of part-time workers in all the countries studied (almost 50% in the Netherlands).

It should be pointed out that the banking and insurance sector is, proportionately, a minor user of part-time working. As the OECD report comments, "the concentration of part-time jobs in the service sector is partly a reflection of the organization of production:

predictable and temporary fluctuations in demand, for example, compel employers to take on part-timers to supplement their full-time workforce. As a general rule, sectors involved in mass production and with high capital investment tend to rely more on a full-time workforce" (Morse, 1969; Nardone, 1986).

Despite these differences, part-time working is on the increase practically everywhere and in some cases is rising dramatically. This can certainly be put down to a number of reasons. Part-time workers "are not covered by certain regulations and do not enjoy certain fringe benefits, which means that employers pay (in proportion to the total wage bill) lower social security contributions for part-time workers than for full-time employees" (OECD, 1986 and Kravaritou, 1987). As we have already seen, part-time workers are employed in sectors where there can be very considerable fluctuations in demand and in these cases they are effectively the flexible element in the organization of labour. Lastly, in difficult periods employers may propose heavy reductions in working hours to avoid dismissals, a policy which has in fact been the subject of a number of company agreements over the past few years. In this last case, demand does not necessarily correspond to supply and it is more a question of forced part-time working. There is however a supply of part-time work which corresponds to the wishes of a section (less extensive than one might think, depending on the country) of the working population (either female or male).

If part-time jobs are clearly identifiable, the same cannot be said of <u>temporary jobs</u>.

The term conceals a multitude of forms and situations which differ depending on the country and legal and institutional contexts involved. It can cover seasonal work, casual labour, fixed-term contracts, supply work, etc. The figures given here come from a survey of the working population (and not of firms) and should therefore be interpreted with some caution.

Temporary jobs as a proportion of total salaried employment by sector, 1983 and 1985[a] (in %)

	All sectors	Agriculture, forestry, fisheries & hunting	Energy & water	Mining industries & chemical products	Manufacturing industries
Belgium					
1983	5.4	7.2	1.9	2.3	2.8
1985	6.9	3.7	3.4	2.4	3.4
Denmark					
1983	-	-	-	-	-
1985	12.3	19.7	3.4	7.2	9.4
France					
1983	3.3	5.1	2.4	2.1	3.7
1985	4.8	7.6	2.5	3.2	4.3
Ireland					
1983	6.2	7.8	3.0	2.2	2.2
1985	7.3	10.4	6.8	5.2	3.8
Italy					
1983	6.6	35.9	2.3	0.9	2.2
1985	4.7	23.9	1.6	0.7	2.0
Japan[b]					
1983	10.3	26.5	2.8	0.0	8.9
1985	10.4	27.9	3.0	0.0	9.1
Luxembourg					
1983	2.6	14.3	0.0	0.6	1.4
1985	5.0	30.0	9.1	2.4	4.1
Netherlands					
1983	5.8	10.1	3.4	1.8	3.1
1985	7.5	-	-	-	-
United Kingdom					
1983	5.5	11.6	1.9	2.3	2.6
1985	5.7	10.6	2.0	2.1	2.9

	Building & public works	Distribution trade	Transport & communications	Banking, insurance, property & services for firms	Other services	Public administration
Belgium						
1983	2.6	6.9	2.7	4.0	9.3	8.2
1985	3.2	6.7	3.1	6.1	12.2	11.6
Denmark						
1983	-	-	-	-	-	-
1985	15.7	15.7	7.1	7.1	13.7	14.4
France						
1983	5.2	6.0	1.1	3.8	2.4	0.7
1985	6.2	6.5	1.9	5.1	5.2	3.9
Ireland						
1983	8.0	7.2	4.1	6.6	10.3	3.0
1985	7.4	8.1	4.1	12.1	10.8	2.8
Italy						
1983	11.9	7.0	1.5	2.0	6.5	2.3
1985	7.0	5.7	1.3	1.9	5.8	2.0
Japan[b]						
1983	17.5	13.4	4.2	3.6	9.9	6.7
1985	16.4	13.5	4.3	3.5	10.2	6.0
Luxembourg						
1983	3.4	3.9	2.2	0.9	4.5	2.5
1985	4.9	7.7	2.2	2.3	7.2	2.6
Netherlands						
1983	3.9	4.9	3.6	3.6	10.0	5.1
1985	-	-	-	-	-	-
United Kingdom						
1983	6.9	10.2	2.2	3.8	7.9	3.9
1985	6.2	8.0	2.2	4.0	8.9	5.2

a. The figures refer to salaried employees only. In all cases, people who have not stated their situation are excluded. With the exception of the UK, the number of people who had not stated their situation was fairly low. For the UK, a considerable number of people in temporary jobs failed to state in which sector they were working; more than 90% were young people aged under 20.

b. The figures are annual averages calculated on the basis of monthly surveys of the working population. Temporary workers include temporary salaried staff - ie people employed for a period of at least one month but less than a year - and day workers - ie people employed on a daily basis or for a period of less than a month. The Japanese classification of sectors of activity is slightly different from the NACE system used in EEC countries: services provided to firms are included under "Other services" and public administration comes under administrative services, not classified elsewhere.

Sources: See Table 1.5 for all countries except Japan and the Netherlands. The figures for Japan are taken from the Annual report on the survey of the working population, Statistical Office, Management and Co-ordination Department. The figures for the Netherlands were provided by Eurostat.

This table prompts two main comments:

1. Temporary work is a growing phenomenon everywhere except in Italy.

2. Except in the case of Denmark, the proportion of temporary workers is still fairly low.

The table also indicates that temporary jobs are heavily concentrated in two sectors - agriculture and the service sector (trade, distribution and other services) - and are uncommon in the manufacturing sector.

The demographic composition of temporary workers is also significant: they tend to be young. The proportion of young temporary workers ranges from 31% to 63% in France; on the other hand, and unlike part-time work, temporary jobs are divided almost equally between men and women.

Demographic composition of temporary workers[a]

(in %)

	Total	Aged 15-24[b]	Aged 25-54	Aged 55+	Men	Women
Belgium, 1985	100.0 (100.0)	47.4 (15.5)	50.5 (77.5)	2.1 (7.0)	44.8 (65.2)	55.2 (34.8)
Denmark, 1985	100.0 (100.0)	62.8 (23.1)	33.3 (66.6)	3.9 (10.3)	50.2 (53.2)	49.8 (46.8)
France, 1985	100.0 (100.0)	62.9 (15.6)	35.5 (77.5)	1.6 (6.9)	58.7 (57.5)	41.3 (42.5)
Ireland, 1985	100.0 (100.0)	58.3 (30.0)	37.8 (61.6)	3.9 (8.4)	48.9 (64.6)	51.1 (35.4)
Italy, 1985	100.0 (100.0)	30.8 (15.3)	57.6 (75.4)	11.6 (9.3)	50.9 (66.5)	49.1 (33.5)
Japan, 1985[c]	100.0 (100.0)	16.0 (15.2)	66.4 (72.6)	17.6 (12.2)	32.3 (64.1)	67.7 (35.9)
Luxembourg, 1985	100.0 (100.0)	65.6 (23.0)	34.4 (61.5)	0.0 (5.5)	49.2 (66.0)	50.8 (34.0)
United Kingdom, 1985	100.0 (100.0)	51.1 (22.1)	41.3 (64.8)	8.6 (13.1)	45.3 (56.2)	54.7 (43.8)
USA, 1985[d]	100.0 (100.0)	32.7 (20.1)	57.6 (67.4)	9.7 (12.5)	35.8 (55.0)	64.2 (45.0)

a. The bracketed figures indicate the demographic composition of all employees. Those who failed to state their situation as regards temporary work have not been taken into account.

b. The figures for Belgium and Italy relate to young people aged 14-24, while those for the UK and the USA relate to young people aged 16-24.

c. Covers only sectors other than agriculture.

d. The figures for the USA are taken from the May 1985 supplement to the Current Population Survey. This supplement included a separate classification for people who considered their jobs to be temporary and whose wages were paid by an employment agency. The figures are therefore not strictly comparable with those given for the other countries here. Furthermore, they do not take account of those permanently employed by employment agencies nor, we suspect, of workers who do not consider their jobs to be temporary because they have fairly regular contact with the employment agency that places them in jobs.

Sources: See Tables 1.5 and 1.8 (Japan). For the USA, see Howe, 1986.

Another distinguishing feature of temporary work revealed by the survey of workers is that people in full-time jobs think of them as permanent. By contrast, people in part-time jobs think of them as temporary; this is true of 11% of part-timers in Denmark and nearly 50% in Italy.

Proportion of workers in permanent or temporary jobs, depending on whether they work full-time or part-time[a]

	Percentage of workers in:			Percentage of workers in:		
	Full-time jobs (thousands)	Permanent jobs	Temporary jobs	Part-time jobs (thousands)	Permanent jobs	Temporary jobs
Belgium						
1983	2 556.5	95.9	4.1	230.6	80.5	19.5
1985	2 549.8	94.7	5.3	259.9	77.4	22.6
Denmark						
1983	-	-	-	-	-	-
1985	1 645.5	87.3	12.7	564.8	88.7	11.3
France						
1983	16 047.7	96.8	3.2	1 579.6	95.7	4.3
1985	15 751.3	95.7	4.3	1 853.0	90.9	9.1
Ireland						
1983	786.3	96.5	3.5	48.0	50.8	49.1
1985	748.6	95.2	4.8	46.5	53.1	46.9
Italy						
1983	14 104.7	95.1	4.9	513.3	45.9	54.1
1985	13 897.6	97.8	2.2	655.4	57.2	42.8
Japan[b]						
1983	36 650.0	93.7	6.3	4 330.0	57.3	42.7
1985	37 460.0	93.8	6.2	4 710.0	57.7	42.3
Luxembourg						
1983	116.6	98.2	1.8	7.6	85.5	14.5
1985	119.6	98.0	2.0	9.4	56.4	43.6
Netherlands						
1983	3 410.3	96.2	3.8	893.5	86.6	13.4
1985	3 467.6	94.7	5.3	996.1	85.0	15.0
UK						
1983	16 587.4	96.9	3.1	4 028.5	84.8	15.2
1985	16 483.9	97.0	3.0	4 565.2	84.0	16.0

a. These figures do not take account of people who did not state their situation.

b. These figures relate only to workers in sectors other than agriculture who were working during the week covered by the survey.

Sources: See Tables 1.5 and 1.8 (Japan and the Netherlands).

The first conclusion to be drawn from all these figures is that these "atypical" forms of work are less widespread than the literature on the subject would lead us to believe. Part-time work has certainly increased considerably in some countries but not in all, and temporary work still represents only a small proportion of total employment.

On the other hand, we can immediately see that there is a very strong tendency for these forms of work to affect particular categories of the labour force - namely young people and women - and that this is not without its drawbacks.

Proponents of quantitative flexibility look no further than the statistics to defend their point of view, but surely we should be looking beyond mere statistics?

... as seen dynamically

In order truly to grasp the significance of the phenomenon, we have in fact to consider the figures dynamically rather than statically.

Between 1983 and 1985, overall employment contracted in France, Ireland and Italy. In France and Italy, this can be fully accounted for by a drop in full-time work; by contrast, the number of part-time jobs increased over the same period. In the UK, about three quarters of the net growth in employment was due to the increase in part-time jobs. In Belgium and Luxembourg, the rise in the number of full-time jobs was the main reason for net growth in employment but, in both these countries, the share of part-time work in the net creation of jobs was greater than the initial proportion of part-time jobs (OECD, 1987).

As the following table indicates, in countries where part-time work has been the principal source of overall growth in employment, as is the case in France, Italy, the Netherlands and the UK, most of the job gains in individual sectors can also be put down to part-time work.

Share of full-time and part-time work in percentage changes in employment by sector between 1983 and 1985[a]
(in %)

	All sectors	Agriculture, forestry, fisheries & hunting	Energy & water	Mining industries & chemical products	Iron & steel & engineering industries	Other manufacturing industries
Belgium						
Total change	2.8	10.4	1.4	-5.7	-2.5	0.9
Share of:						
full-time work	2.0	8.8	1.1	-5.4	-2.1	0.3
part-time work	0.8	1.6	0.3	-0.3	-0.4	0.6
Employment in 1983 (thousands)	3 414.6	114.9	63.1	202.7	301.4	369.0
France						
Total change	-0.4	-3.3	9.9	-2.3	-6.3	0.8
Share of:						
full-time work	-1.5	-1.8	9.2	-2.7	-5.3	0.5
part-time work	1.1	-1.5	0.7	0.4	-1.0	0.3
Employment in 1983 (thousands)	21 204.5	1 783.8	281.7	798.0	2 238.1	2 060.1
Ireland						
Total change	-4.7	-10.2	-1.2	-0.3	-3.6	-10.4
Share of:						
full-time work	-4.2	-7.8	-0.6	0.3	-2.7	-9.4
part-time work	-0.5	-2.4	-0.6	-0.6	-0.9	-1.0
Employment in 1983 (thousands)	1 117.5	195.6	16.5	38.1	63.5	125.6
Italy						
Total change	-0.1	-8.6	-1.8	-8.3	-9.0	-6.6
Share of:						
full-time work	-0.8	-8.4	-2.8	-8.7	-9.2	-7.1
part-time work	0.7	-0.2	1.0	0.4	0.2	0.5
Employment in 1983 (thousands)	20 583.0	2 465.7	206.7	692.6	1 690.1	2 734.4
Luxembourg						
Total change	3.0	-2.9	-31.3	4.4	18.0	-6.6
Share of:						
full-time work	2.2	0.0	-31.3	3.8	14.0	-6.6
part-time work	0.8	-2.9	0.0	0.6	4.0	0.0
Employment in 1983 (thousands)	142.1	6.9	1.6	16.0	5.0	10.6
Netherlands[b]						
Total change	4.5	-1.6		5.6		
Share of:						
full-time work	1.4	-1.3		1.2		
part-time work	3.1	-0.3		4.4		
Employment in 1983 (thousands)	4 820.7	267.7		981.5		
United Kingdom						
Total change	4.2	-3.3	-8.0	-8.1	-1.6	6.0
Share of:						
full-time work	1.1	-5.7	-7.4	-7.7	-1.6	3.6
part-time work	3.1	2.4	-0.6	-0.4	0.0	2.4
Employment in 1983 (thousands)	22 904.9	582.3	749.4	850.8	2 588.9	2 338.5

	Building & public works	Distribution trade	Transport & communications	Banking, insurance, property & services for firms	Other services	Public administration
Belgium						
Total change	-4.7	4.8	-1.9	9.3	6.3	5.6
Share of:						
full-time work	-5.2	4.1	-2.2	8.5	5.4	2.6
part-time work	0.5	0.7	0.3	0.8	0.9	3.0
Employment in 1983 (thousands)	207.0	631.4	268.4	228.7	711.5	316.5
France						
Total change	-7.1	-3.2	1.1	0.3	5.4	4.6
Share of:						
full-time work	-7.4	-4.3	-0.3	-1.4	2.4	0.8
part-time work	0.3	1.1	1.4	1.7	3.0	3.8
Employment in 1983 (thousands)	1 678.2	3 641.0	1 267.4	1 614.0	4 047.8	1 794.4
Ireland						
Total change	-8.3	2.4	-7.0	-3.6	-3.2	-5.4
Share of:						
full-time work	-7.3	2.6	-7.0	-4.2	-4.4	-5.1
part-time work	-1.0	-0.2	0.0	0.6	1.2	-0.3
Employment in 1983 (thousands)	97.9	197.5	59.9	81.0	174.9	67.0
Italy						
Total change	-5.6	4.3	-3.0	14.7	-2.2	34.5
Share of:						
full-time work	-6.2	3.1	-3.2	13.9	-3.0	33.1
part-time work	0.6	1.2	0.2	0.8	0.8	1.4
Employment in 1983 (thousands)	2 088.5	4 140.8	1 126.2	636.0	3 218.2	1 583.8
Luxembourg						
Total change	2.3	0.3	0.0	18.6	8.5	-5.0
Share of:						
full-time work	-0.8	-1.0	-1.1	16.9	8.1	-4.2
part-time work	3.1	1.3	1.1	1.7	0.4	-0.8
Employment in 1983 (thousands)	13.0	30.0	9.3	11.8	25.8	12.1
Netherlands[b]						
Total change	1.4	0.9	c	8.9	3.5	2.4
Share of:						
full-time work	0.4	-1.0	c	4.2	-2.7	1.7
part-time work	1.0	1.9	c	4.7	6.2	0.7
Employment in 1983 (thousands)	377.6	884.7		414.6	888.6	755.3
United Kingdom						
Total change	2.2	3.5	-2.2	19.2	14.5	-12.3
Share of:						
full-time work	0.2	0.2	-2.6	15.4	6.4	-12.5
part-time work	2.0	3.3	0.6	3.8	8.1	0.2
Employment in 1983 (thousands)	1 734.9	4 617.7	1 474.1	1 846.5	4 640.0	1 481.8

a. The figures cover everyone in employment, except for those who could not be classified because it was not known whether they had part-time or full-time jobs or in which sector of activity they were employed.

b. The figures for the Netherlands are based on the SBI system for the classification of sectors of activity. They refer only to those people whose working hours were specified (see note a. to Table 1.3).

c. In 1983, more than 20% of all employees in this sector were not classified according to their working hours, as against less than 2% in 1985. It is therefore impossible to calculate with any precision the contributions of full-time and part-time work. Employment in this sector is however included under the column heading "All sectors".

Sources: The figures for the Netherlands were provided by the Ministry for Social Affairs and Employment. Figures for the other countries were supplied by Eurostat and are based on the results of national surveys on the labour force.

As regards temporary work, the following table indicates the occupational situation of permanent or temporary workers as it was a year previously.

The occupational situation of permanent or temporary workers a year previously

	\multicolumn{5}{c}{Occupational situation a year previously}
Current situation & country	Total	Salaried staff	Other categories of workers	Unemployed	Non-workers
Belgium, 1985					
Permanent job	100.0	95.6	0.3	1.8	2.3
Temporary job	100.0	58.5	0.4	18.0	23.1
Denmark, 1985					
Permanent job	100.0	94.1	0.2	2.6	3.1
Temporary job	100.0	68.1	0.3	13.4	18.2
France, 1985					
Permanent job	100.0	94.0	0.5	2.4	3.1
Temporary job	100.0	48.2	1.0	19.4	31.4
Ireland, 1985					
Permanent job	100.0	94.0	0.6	2.5	2.9
Temporary job	100.0	50.4	0.5	19.4	29.7
Italy, 1983					
Permanent job	100.0	94.4	1.2	2.1	2.3
Temporary job	100.0	71.8	0.9	15.5	17.8
Luxembourg, 1985					
Permanent job	100.0	95.4	0.2	1.2	3.2
Temporary job	100.0	70.0	0.0	3.3	26.7
Netherlands, 1985					
Permanent job	100.0	95.3	0.1	1.4	3.2
Temporary job	100.0	61.6	0.9	12.7	24.8
United Kingdom, 1985					
Permanent job	100.0	91.0	1.7	2.5	4.8
Temporary job	100.0	48.5	6.2	14.2	31.1

Sources: See Tables 1.5 and 1.8 (Netherlands)

At the time of the survey, more than 90% of those who said they had a permanent job had been salaried employees a year previously. Those who said they had temporary jobs had, in varying proportions depending on the country concerned, been unemployed or not working; this is particularly the case in the United Kingdom and France.

These findings suggest that access to permanent employment is becoming increasingly difficult and that, in a number of countries, temporary work is now the normal route out of unemployment or occupational inactivity (in France, temporary jobs account for 80% of annual recruitment) and the only way to enter working life.

Very little information is available on "exits" from temporary work and it would be very useful to know whether a move out of a temporary job necessarily implies a move into a permanent post. A survey conducted in the Netherlands (OJA, 1987) reveals that almost 56% of workers in temporary jobs in May 1985 held permanent posts by October 1986, though some 37% were still in temporary jobs and 7% were unemployed.

A series of surveys have also been conducted on the beneficiaries of community manpower schemes (Piotet, 1987) in Germany, the UK and France. Here too, it has to be admitted that these jobs only occasionally lead to permanent employment.

Temporary jobs may be a sensible "buffer" between leaving the education system and entering the world of work (Grootings and Stefanov, 1984). They may also meet the wishes of some wage-earners. Today, however, they correspond more to a lasting (?) change in the concept of employment. Looking at the _dynamic_ trends in part-time work and temporary work, what we are actually seeing is employment becoming more precarious.

b) The law and its application

We have attempted to present in as much detail as possible existing data on the best-known figures concerning these new forms of work in order to pinpoint the main lines of the debate, although without making any claim to have given an exhaustive account.

It may be difficult to be precise about the figures but it is easier, even if the task is a complex one, to analyse the relevant regulations, whether they are based on legislation or labour agreements.

Comparative texts on this subject are numerous.

The most recent publication is the study carried out under the direction of Professor Blampain at the request of the Foundation (Blampain, 1987). This study gives a summary of national reports covering all the Member States and bears exclusively on the legal and contractual limitations to working time. It is therefore not a report on current regulations in all the areas concerning new forms of work, but only on those which govern the flexibility of working time.

The main conclusion to be drawn from the report goes some way towards confirming what the figures suggest, ie that the situation differs very widely from country to country, which makes any attempt to introduce Community-wide legislation problematic.

In its conclusion the report, in interpreting the descriptions of the legal situation on the subject, stresses what the author calls "controlled deregulation", two words which are in fact at the centre of a very heated debate. For the report notes a significant relaxation of the rules on the length and organization of working time in every country. But not everyone sees this deregulation as exactly controlled. The report describes current regulations in each country; it does not discuss the effectiveness of the law and its application, but then that was not its intention.

A slightly earlier report, dating from September 1985, which was co-ordinated by J.M. Maury and contains studies on Germany, Belgium, France, Italy, the Netherlands and the UK (and more detailed studies on Ireland and Denmark), attempts among other things to measure the existing gap between the law and practice and deals mainly with the general area of flexibility, not at a theoretical level but as it is conceived or accepted by trade unions, employers and governments.

The author first analyses the underlying attractions of the idea of flexibility and identifies four main reasons for the current debate.

The first lies in the realization that macroeconomic policies are failing to solve the unemployment problem. "Faced with this realization, it is only natural that other paths should be explored, and 'flexibility' appears - perhaps without any real grounds - to be the most promising solution." As J.M. Maury says, "people are not turning to flexibility because it has proved its worth: no large-scale study has shown beyond doubt that flexibility has either a substantial or negligible impact on unemployment". Maury's comment echoes the fresh notoriety being enjoyed by enterprise in all the EEC countries, and particularly in those that had predicted the least favourable fate for it.

The second reason lies in the economic gulf opening up between Europe and its main competitors: the USA and Japan. Here too, whether rightly or wrongly and always on the basis of little practical evidence, these two countries are claimed to owe their success to their very flexible employment systems; that at least appears to be the opinion held by governments and employers' organizations.

The third reason is linked to technological development. This may be grounds for major organizational changes but, at the same time, the financial viability of new technology depends on greater flexibility in its use.

The final reason concerns unemployment itself. The rise in unemployment has helped to weaken trade unions considerably and employers may feel that now is the time to call into question the rights acquired by workers.

Other reasons could be added to those mentioned by the author, particularly those linked with structural changes in employment and the development of the service sector, and perhaps also with changes in workers' expectations.

As well as identifying these reasons, the author attempts to define the main points under debate, some of which touch on the subject of our report and also help to clarify its scope.

"Flexibility takes on a different guise in each country but it may be noted both that it is often seen as a global problem and that a number of common basic themes are apparent.

The principal common areas are: flexibility of pay, flexibility in the organization of working hours, the possibility of using labour with insecure tenure, the removal of obstacles to dismissal, vocational training and threshold effects.

1. Pay

The aims of governments and/or employers vary from country to country. In Italy, the basic problem is to put a stop to the practice of index-linking wages to prices. In the UK, the aim is purely and simply to lower real wages in order to increase employment, according to the well-known neo-classical economic theory. In the Netherlands, the objective is "the redistribution of work" via a reduction in working hours with little or no pay compensation. Elsewhere, the situation is more varied: the objectives outlined above are apparent, together with the demand for a starting wage for young people which is lower than the legal or contractually agreed minimum wage, and a tendency towards the increased individualization of pay.

2. Organization of working time

There is strong pressure to make the organization of working time more flexible, ie to allow on the one hand for considerable irregularity in working hours from one week to the next and, on the other, for the development of shiftwork and weekend shifts. In Germany, the Netherlands and France, the problem seems to arise mainly in connection with the reduction of working time. The problem of reducing and reorganizing working hours gives rise to a further problem: that of the level of negotiation.

Objectively, it would appear most sensible to discuss this kind of problem at company level, yet in most countries negotiation systems centre on the branch or even the region. This has led to some questioning of the issue, which threatens to be heavy with consequences (the problem is particularly acute in Germany and France).

3. Part-time working, temporary jobs and fixed-term contracts
There is some movement in this direction in every country but no spectacular development would appear to be on the cards. The trend is moderate but should be noted and observed, whether it is towards part-time working (France and Belgium) or temporary jobs and fixed-term contracts (Italy, UK and Belgium).

4. Dismissal
Some relaxation of the constraints on dismissal is being sought in every country, but with varying emphasis and in different forms. It may simply take the form of a change in staffing threshold levels that assure employees some protection against dismissal (Germany); in France, the major topic here is the employers' demand for the abolition of government authorization (for dismissals for financial reasons); in the UK, Belgium and the Netherlands (and also in France), the push is towards a reduction in periods of notice; in Belgium and the UK, trial employment periods are being extended (to 12 or 24 months).

5. Vocational training
Almost every country has introduced programmes to facilitate the integration of young people into working life. Vocational training, whether initial or continuing, is clearly decisive in the introduction and application of new technology.

6. Threshold effects
This problem is common to almost all European countries. It does not bear on a large number of potential jobs but often employer pressure makes it an example of the rigidity of employment conditions. The problem affects growing small and medium-sized enterprises, ie the firms that create most jobs, which gives the problem its psychological significance.

There are other important subjects concerning flexibility but they tend to be country-specific (eg recruitment rigidities in Italy because of job tendering, and the large numbers of people leaving jobs through early retirement in France). The problem of the charges linked with pay is a very important subject but available studies do not allow us to draw any useful conclusions."

Finally, the report attempts to discuss actual practices as regards flexibility. In particular, it reveals that wide margins for flexibility are currently offered by legal and contractual regulations but are not always put to full use. On the other hand, some firms are experimenting widely with flexibility but their efforts go unnoticed by those who are discussing the problem at national level.

It is difficult to judge the impact of flexibility on employment; the effects are not necessarily all negative, but flexibility does involve some potential risks, which will be examined at a later point.

The report commissioned by the Foundation from Professor Kravaritou (Kravaritou, 1987) on new forms of work and activity and their impact on labour and social-security law in the Member States of the European Community concentrates on analysing the effects of the development of new forms of work on labour law. The approach is evidently different from the one followed by Professor Blampain. The aim is not to give an account of the current legal situation but to analyse the progression of events that has led to the transformation of, or increasingly wider departures from, the traditional rules governing employment contracts. It thus happens that "individual employment contracts or company agreements go against some of the general principles of labour law. Worse still, in some countries new legally imposed regulations relating to new forms of work and activity depart from the spirit of the law in re-introducing, sometimes under new names, old and since rejected forms of work dating from the nineteenth century, when labour law was almost non-existent". The author also condemns the development of forms of work that are not covered by labour law and particularly "para-subordinate" (as they are called in Italy) or independent jobs and moonlighting, which have been able to develop partly because employment has become too flexible (see also for this approach in general E. Vogel Polski, 1987).

Without being able to settle the debate once and for all either way, the terms do seem to be clearly expressed.

Labour law is changing and changing rapidly, moving towards a growing relaxation of the constraints imposed on employers.

This "deregulation" is justified by the public authorities under the pretext that flexibility will most closely meet the real needs of firms. National legislation is, by its very nature, unable to cope with the diversity of situations and must therefore be replaced by negotiation between employers and employees at branch and company level; but negotiation has not yet reached the stage where it can bridge the gaps in the law.

Some people in these new forms of work are being discriminated against and enjoy less protection than is afforded to the core of permanent employees within firms.

c) <u>Flexibility in practice</u>

Reports, studies and research papers are all agreed on the wide diversity of economic, legal and institutional situations prevailing in different countries. Very few research reports give us a synoptic and above all comparative view of the very numerous case studies available for each of the Member States. A study of this type has however been conducted for the General Planning Commission in France by the IRIS Research Centre: "Travail et société" (Work and society), under the direction of J.M. Maury (Maury, 1986). This research, which is a continuation of the research work mentioned earlier, compares the practices of 26 Italian, German, French, British and Belgian firms as regards flexibility. In view of its size, the sample could hardly be said to be representative.

The firms were in fact selected because flexibility played an important or even decisive role for them. It was also decided to select mainly medium-sized enterprises because "very large firms deal with the problem of flexibility in too specific a manner (they possess very substantial resources and have a special relationship with the public authorities)".

Before presenting the findings, it should be pointed out that this study uses a functional definition of flexibility: "employment flexibility covers all those measures that substantially modify employees' conditions of employment in order to enable the firm to adapt to its environment and particularly to its market".

The results of the survey are summarized by the author as follows:

The financial problems encountered are several:

- adjusting to changes in demand, which may be growing, contracting, cyclical or simply irregular:
    in our sample, we observed 58% of cases with irregular or cyclical demand and 27% of cases with contracting demand;

- improving price competitivity by cutting costs via capital savings, productivity gains and a lowering of the reject rate (or of the cost of internal non-quality):
    58% of the firms studied need to increase the useful life of their machinery; 42% need to improve productivity, 26% of them by staff cuts;

- improving quality competitivity (quality in the external sense):
    quality is a problem for 58% of the firms;

- modifying the product or product range:
    38% of the firms studied have had to modify their product range (reduction: 3, diversification: 3, complete change: 3, specialization: 1);

- introducing new technology as a consequence of the above:
    this is the case in 84% of the firms studied.

Flexibility measures observed within the sample may be classified as follows:

a) Organization of working time

- annual organization with possible overtime:
    58% of the firms use various methods to vary working times depending on the period concerned;

- weekly organization via the formation of shift crews:
  several configurations appear:
    * 2 x 8 or 3 x 8 shifts over 5 days;
    * 3 x 8 or 3 x 6 shifts over 6 days;
    * 3 x 8 shifts over 7 days;
    * weekend shifts (associated with 3 x 8 or 2 x 8 shifts);
    * day-specific shifts.
    In our sample, 73% of firms use this type of weekly organization (two of which use continuous shifts), often combining various configurations;

- in some cases, the introduction of shiftwork has been accompanied by a reduction in working hours:
    23% of the sample.

b) Job reorganization

- internal occupational mobility:
    50% of the sample;

- development of multi-skilling:
    50%;

- training:
    69% are making a very substantial effort as regards training (usually in connection with occupational mobility and multi-skilling);

- quality circles:
    formal quality circles are used in only three of the sample firms but some of the others operate similar methods to encourage workers to help improve quality.

c) <u>Differential status</u>

- partial unemployment (or similar legal forms):
    23% of the sample (ie use of the Cassa Integrazione in Italy, whereby the Government makes up the pay of laid-off workers);

- part-time working:
    23%;

- temporary and fixed-term contracts:
    23%;

- "employment/training" contracts:
    23%.

d) <u>Staff cuts</u>

- early retirement:
    27%;

- mass redundancies:
    1 firm;

- resignations:
    3 firms (essentially involving resignations prompted by special incentives).

e) <u>Pay flexibility</u>

- individual bonuses (productivity, quality, other):
    27% of the sample;

- collective bonuses (productivity, quality, other):
    46%;

- profit-sharing:
    2 firms.

These findings are interesting in that they illustrate two types of flexibility:

. a flexibility which consists in adapting to the volume of work: altering, reorganizing or reducing working time and/or recourse to special forms of employment such as temporary and fixed-term contracts, part-time working or employment/training contracts;

. a flexibility which consists in manipulating the skill status of work, the multi-skilling of the workforce and, of course, their motivation.

These practical findings confirm the more general analyses of flexibility as a multi-faceted phenomenon, which will be examined later.

The report also examines the methods of introducing flexibility within an enterprise. The conclusions that can be drawn are limited by the fact that the sample included only "firms in which there was a union presence and real bargaining activity". This may be the norm in some countries but it is generally more of an exception, particularly in small and medium-sized enterprises.

With these reservations, the report notes that only most of the measures concerning the reorganization of working time give rise to negotiation in French and Belgian firms, whereas all of the measures concerning flexibility are negotiated in Italian and British firms. (This matter is also discussed in the recent ILO report on flexibility, which provides numerous examples of company agreements in European countries.) It is to be regretted that no comparable information is available on the flexibility strategies followed by large firms, whose policies, whether real or presumed, are the basis of the most predictive analyses of flexibility.

II. Predictions

The line dividing description and prediction, which we shall attempt to draw here, is uncertain and always being overlapped. In view of what we have already stated in the first part of this report, the reasons for this are evident. New forms of work and the debate on flexibility are still young and very precise quantitative data for analysis are more often than not lacking. This means that a very large number of publications are really half-way between description and prediction and it is doubtless this uncertainty over their status which rouses such heated controversies.

a) From the boundaries of description...

Some of the reports and researches analysed earlier include a section whose development rests on a series of "reasonable" hypotheses regarding the possible consequences of new forms of work. These hypotheses may be considered as strictly ideological viewpoints and, as such, rejected or discounted; however, as they have been formulated by experts or researchers with long experience, they are undoubtedly worth taking into consideration and should not in any case be underestimated: the worst may not happen, but sometimes it does.

A first example of this approach is provided by the publications of J.M. Maury when he evokes the risks inherent in policies that destabilize employment. For Maury, there are five essential risks:

Risk 1: distortion of competition
Instead of proving their ability to compete by introducing technical and organizational innovations, firms may content themselves with resorting to a temporary workforce or "concertinaed" working hours.

Risk 2: weakening of proper labour management by firms
If firms can recruit and dismiss staff at will, what incentive will they have to develop a foward-looking labour management policy? This cannot fail to have far-reaching effects on employment and the employability of the unemployed.

Risk 3: demotivation of workers
Can workers reasonably be expected to be committed to their work if they feel that their jobs are always insecure? Does not work motivation also depend on the level of social protection afforded?

Risk 4: further segmentation of the labour market
The relaxation of employment regulations will not necessarily lead to greater equality among wage-earners by abolishing the privileges of the few and levelling down employment status. On the contrary, as some research work has already indicated, the risk is that some groups will experience even greater job instability while others will be able to consolidate their already strong positions.

Risk 5: devaluation of the labour force
Or rather, devaluation of the under-utilized part of the labour force.

Many more examples of such analyses can be found in the Foundation's publication on new forms of work and activity (Brussels Colloquium, 1986). These examples bear on the psychological impact of new forms of work on the individual (Renda and Reuter), or on family life and the social system (Piotet). These hypotheses are based on practical experience. For instance, a French survey on atypical working hours (weekend working, the compressed working week, night working, alternating shiftwork, Saturday or Sunday working and irregular cycles) (P. Boisard and F. Guelaud, 1987) concentrates on analysing the impact of these working hours on:

- changes in day-to-day activities: housework and shopping, visits to administrative, medical and educational bodies, etc;

- changes in family life: time spent with the family, spouse and children;

- changes in leisure activities and the use of free time;

- possible repercussions on health.

The results of this research corroborate the hypotheses put forward: atypical working hours make men's lives easier, provided their wives are not out at work too, but they always complicate women's lives. In most cases, they affect social life in its widest sense and a third of those questioned said that atypical working hours caused psychological problems and particularly difficulty in sleeping. The time freed by working atypical hours may make the worker feel less fraught but it also makes friendships and human relationships in general more difficult. These findings are however more optimistic than those obtained by research conducted in other countries (Staines and Pleck, 1984) and particularly in the USA, which shows that atypical working hours lead to more problems and conflicts in family life, even though they enable workers to devote more time to their families. The Foundation's studies on the impact of shiftwork on all aspects of life are highly illustrative of all the problems that have been mentioned here.

One of the objections often levelled against these atypical forms of work is that they are not randomly distributed among the entire working population but seem to be reserved for particular groups and refused to others. Thus, as we have already seen, part-time work is essentially a female domain. It is, however, <u>young people</u> who are being most affected by these precarious forms of employment.

This question is dealt with in the proceedings of two European seminars held respectively at Sofia in 1984 (Grootings and Stefanov) and at Marseilles in September 1987 (they are mentioned here because, apart from their own contributions, they provide a summary of the enormous quantity of work undertaken on this subject in Europe).

The papers presented at the Sofia colloquium consider the integration of young people into the world of work in a context of rapid technological change. They point to the very wide gap which appears to exist in every European country between young people's expectations and the jobs available to them. Above all, they show that it has become more and more difficult for young people to enter working life and that no young person today, whatever his or her level of training, is safe from unemployment or, consequently, from the risk of being sucked into the network of unstable forms of work.

Even though these atypical forms of work were already developing rapidly in the early 1980s, it is significant that studies on young people at the time were mainly concerned with the trend towards jobs associated with technological change rather than with the precariousness of employment. The very recent conference on this theme, which was held in Marseilles under the aegis of the Commission of the European Communities, shows how much concerns have changed over a very short period. Technological change has given way to flexibility, which is now the centre of the debate. We shall now quote from the summary report presented by J.R. Pendaries, which deals specifically with flexibility.

"We are all aware of the importance acquired by the theme of flexibility in economic discourses over the past ten years, particularly in the OECD countries, and it comes as no surprise to find it playing a prominent role in the Community's approach to the economic crisis, an approach in which it functions on two fronts: the analysis of the underlying factors and reasons for this crisis and of its possible development and effects.

This is particularly clear in the approach to questions concerning young people, which from a macroeconomic point of view refer to phenomena such as the collapse of economic growth, changes in production methods and international competition, and the development of new technology, with all its potential repercussions, particularly on the general contraction of job vacancies. Furthermore, these multiple causes are accompanied and aggravated by certain functional features of the labour market, and in such a way that specific categories of the labour force suffer the worst effects, with young people in the front line.

In other words, the youth question is dependent on macroeconomic dynamics 'under the mediation' of certain features of the job market: 'it would seem that regulations or collective agreements on minimum wages may (particularly when the minimum wage is relatively close to the average wage) have the effect of damaging the job prospects of precisely those categories of workers whom these provisions are supposed to protect, particularly young people. If collective agreements are negotiated without sufficient differentiation according to age, experience and productivity, they too may have a negative effect. It would appear that certain features of current practice and legislation as regards employment, for example provisions governing recruitment, training, working hours and dismissal, may have prejudicial effects for the long-term unemployed, particularly for low-skilled workers, newcomers on the labour market and people seeking jobs with flexible or reduced working hours'.

So we have a broad area for reflection, where the youth question is associated with the problem of the rigidity/fluidity of the job market. 'Young people are suffering disproportionately from the contraction in the number of jobs owing to the alteration in the traditional structure of recruitment and the rotation of the workforce. (...) Worsening circumstances naturally tend mainly to penalize the least protected and competitive categories of workers as well as new arrivals on the job market. (...) Today, it is young people who are bearing the brunt of the fluctuation' (idem). In brief, young people are paying a heavier price than their elders for the labour market's inflexibilities and the youth question, in as far as it is a unique and specific problem, is therefore closely linked to the problem of the rigidity/flexibility of the job market.

It should firstly be noted that the problem of flexibility suggests a somewhat wider perspective than the approach in terms of segmentation. The latter may well have a decisive contribution to make to the former in allowing us to identify the various "rigidity" factors of the job market, but for this very reason it would appear difficult for such an approach to be sensitive to, and take account of, a group of phenomena which, by contrast and primarily, are at the centre of the flexibility problem; that is, those phenomena which have been growing ever since the late 1960s and become apparent in the various <u>forms of crisis and destabilization affecting relations, regulations, agreements and status which are a functional feature of the labour market</u>. Thus, where an approach in terms of segmentation will, as we have seen above, examine the new methods of managing the transition to adulthood from the point of view of the new forms of differentiation and stratification of the labour market that they imply, the approach in terms of 'flexibilization' will, by contrast, stress the 'scrambling' that they tend to cause in the traditional and trenchant rigidity of the distinctions between, say, student, apprentice and worker. More generally, and without necessarily disputing the segmentation theories, the approach in terms of flexibilization is distinguished by the dynamic, evolutive and forward-looking viewpoint that it implies.

This is, in our opinion, a relatively important point with regard to the youth question because it would appear that it is by this type of approach that Community measures can most explicitly and thoroughly place youth problems in the context of the short-, medium- and long-term development of our societies. This is particularly true when it comes to questions of training.

On this point, the main features of the approach can be summarized as follows:

- 'Unlike during the 1970s, young people today are urged to pursue their training and preparation for adult life beyond compulsory schooling.'
- 'Since, in overall terms, the number of young people looking for full-time jobs as soon as they have finished their compulsory schooling is tending to fall in most Member States, the importance of the "threshold" represented by the end of compulsory schooling is diminishing, and all the more so since "special measures" for the young unemployed are increasingly being integrated within the Member States' general education and vocational training structures or are presented as "transitional steps" between education and training within firms.'
- More generally, through the extension of initial training to the age of 18, it is the period of transition as a whole which is being lengthened. Insertion into the world of work is no longer a 'single moment', rather it is a multitude of points of entry and exit to be negotiated by youngsters, which often puts them in a complex and confusing situation. This tends to call into question the representation and even the status of young people as 'the traditional distinction between "employment" and "unemployment" becomes less and less apt, both as a description of what governments are trying to do (or are avoiding doing) and as a description of everyday life as it is lived by young people.'
- So what we have been experiencing is 'an important change in vocabulary since 1982/83. At that time, many governments were simply trying to offer young people without work a constructive alternative to unemployment. It is now being more and more widely admitted that

high youth unemployment is likely to continue for a long time yet and that, in order to remain successfully competitive on world markets, the Community needs a flexible, highly trained workforce'. It is within this framework that 'measures which were originally introduced essentially as a short-term response to growing unemployment among young people will have to become a permanent fixture'.

To jump from there to the belief that the youth question seen from this point of view is a rich field of experimentation for a more global flexibilization strategy is a step that, as we have seen (cf Farnham Castle), only a few people take. For our part, we would at least maintain that, whatever the ideological and political ins and outs, the problem of flexibility functions here as a powerful (or the most powerful) vehicle for putting the youth question into perspective in terms of the social stakes involved, which go far beyond it, and allows us to interpret its various aspects, including the most 'cyclical', in the light of the major changes in our societies. That, in our eyes, is the only interest of such an approach.

That said, a few comments need to be made. The first is that there are no grounds for believing that what we have here is a true attempt at analysis: this approach neither constitutes nor proposes <u>any theory</u>. The fact that the references that we have just used are all drawn from documents and not from Community studies is significant in itself: it would appear that no Community study has been commissioned to tackle the youth question from this viewpoint. When it is mentioned, it is usually only in a marginal way, as a <u>preliminary and generalized theme</u>, whose content and details are only ever ever touched on. Thus the question only comes up when reflection on wage differentials between adults and young people stumbles against its own inadequacies and suggests a widening of the field of analysis to cover all forms of regulation and deregulation in labour relations (see particularly the way in which the Dutch national agreement signed by the social partners in 1982 constitutes for D. Marsden, for example, a kind of model for approaching these questions).

The interest of the approach seems in fact to lie elsewhere: in its capacity to bring together, converging on a precise topic of study, a whole combination of analyses and data issuing from many fields of concern and research which are usually isolated from each other and to which attempts are made to apply a relatively coherent pattern of interpretation. Thus at the centre of this convergence we invariably find the theme of <u>modes and conceptions of human existence</u>, particularly from the point of view of the place occupied in it by work: 'given that massive long-term unemployment is likely to become a lasting feature, it is essential to re-examine fundamental questions such as the nature and aims of non-vocational training to provide people with the resources to cope with a prolonged period of occupational inactivity.' Furthermore, it is 'future modes of existence and work' which are in question here and 'this difficult period could be an ideal opportunity to remove the distinction between employment and unemployment.'

Yet this leads on to a second comment on the contours and contents of this 'thematic convergence'. We should in fact like to draw attention to the fact that the flexibility in question here is only that flexibility which affects the labour market and, still more precisely, the characteristics of the labour force and the social, legal and contractual conditions of its 'deployment'. All the facets concerning investment policies, the structure of firms and labour relations, methods of technological development, etc, which are an integral part of a full analysis of the crisis (cf the various Community documents already cited), are systematically omitted in an approach in which flexibility is only ever defined as the abilities and conditions according to which the supply of labour adjusts to the demand. Thus when the question of restructuring relationships between education and the economy is discussed, for example, attention is unilaterally focused on education, as it is taken for granted that the problem is to develop 'the personal and social abilities which young people need in order to adapt to change and to the uncertainty of their future prospects.'

A significant omission, also from the point of view of the direction that future policies should take - policies which could for example face 'the question of whether, instead of simply accepting the structure of employment as it is and adapting the labour force to that structure, it would not be better, on the contrary, to take the structure of the labour force as the given quantity and try to match the structure of employment to it. This would give us a qualitative employment policy rather than a labour force policy'. (See "Les concepts de chômage - le chômage structurel [Concepts of unemployment - structural unemployment], Dossiers, No 42, op cit.)

In other words, and even though the perspective could be broadened to take account of far-reaching changes in the very apparatus and mode of production, the approach followed under the theme of flexibilization tends, here too, to contract the field of reflection on youth questions to the admittedly wider but still very narrow field of the labour market alone.

This means that, contrary to its potential, the approach tends to prevent research from trying to discover whether what is at play, through the crisis being suffered by the new generations, does not in fact arise from a generalized conception of the relationship between the individual and the economy, a conception whose crisis may well already date back a long time but whose development has been 'masked throughout the period of economic growth'."

This analysis defines the terms of the debate very clearly. It underlines the important role of public policies in the development of these new forms of work. We shall return to this role in our conclusion, but it is important to make the following comments here:

1. The provisional measures taken by governments to alleviate youth unemployment are likely to turn progressively into permanent measures.

2. The permanence of these measures will gradually contribute to a change in the image of employment. It is going to become the norm to pass through a community manpower scheme before moving on to a more permanent post. Within their sphere of influence, the public authorities are thus helping to create a whole series of atypical jobs which are precarious to varying degrees but which, in many cases, are no longer a contingency remedy.

b) ... to the limits of prediction

On the basis of these descriptions/predictions, researchers have naturally tried to build a theoretical corpus which goes towards confirming "flexibility" as a fact and predicts its future.

- On this theme, and because they are most closely aligned with our subject, we shall cite the publications of Atkinson. This author firstly defines the various facets of flexibility and conveniently distinguishes:

- Numerical flexibility, which consists in adjusting employment in line with demand by using various methods, ranging from the reorganization of working time to all the different forms of temporary work, including subcontracting - the flexible firm is one which always has just the right number of employees, whatever the fluctuations in demand.

- <u>Functional flexibility</u> takes account of the adaptability of employees to qualitative changes in demand. These changes may be induced by the market, by technology or by the strategy options taken by the firm - functional flexibility reveals the skill of the workforce.

- <u>Pay flexibility</u> reflects the manner in which the pay structure supports functional and numerical flexibility. It shows how pay levels are a reflection of individual performance and of the value of a specific skill on the market. It is a means to flexibility rather than an end in itself.

For Atkinson, if these are all the facets of flexibility, its main feature lies in the segmentation which is caused between groups of workers; all workers must be flexible but not in the same way: some serve functional flexibility, others aid numerical flexibility. This can be illustrated by the following diagram, which is often used in the literature.

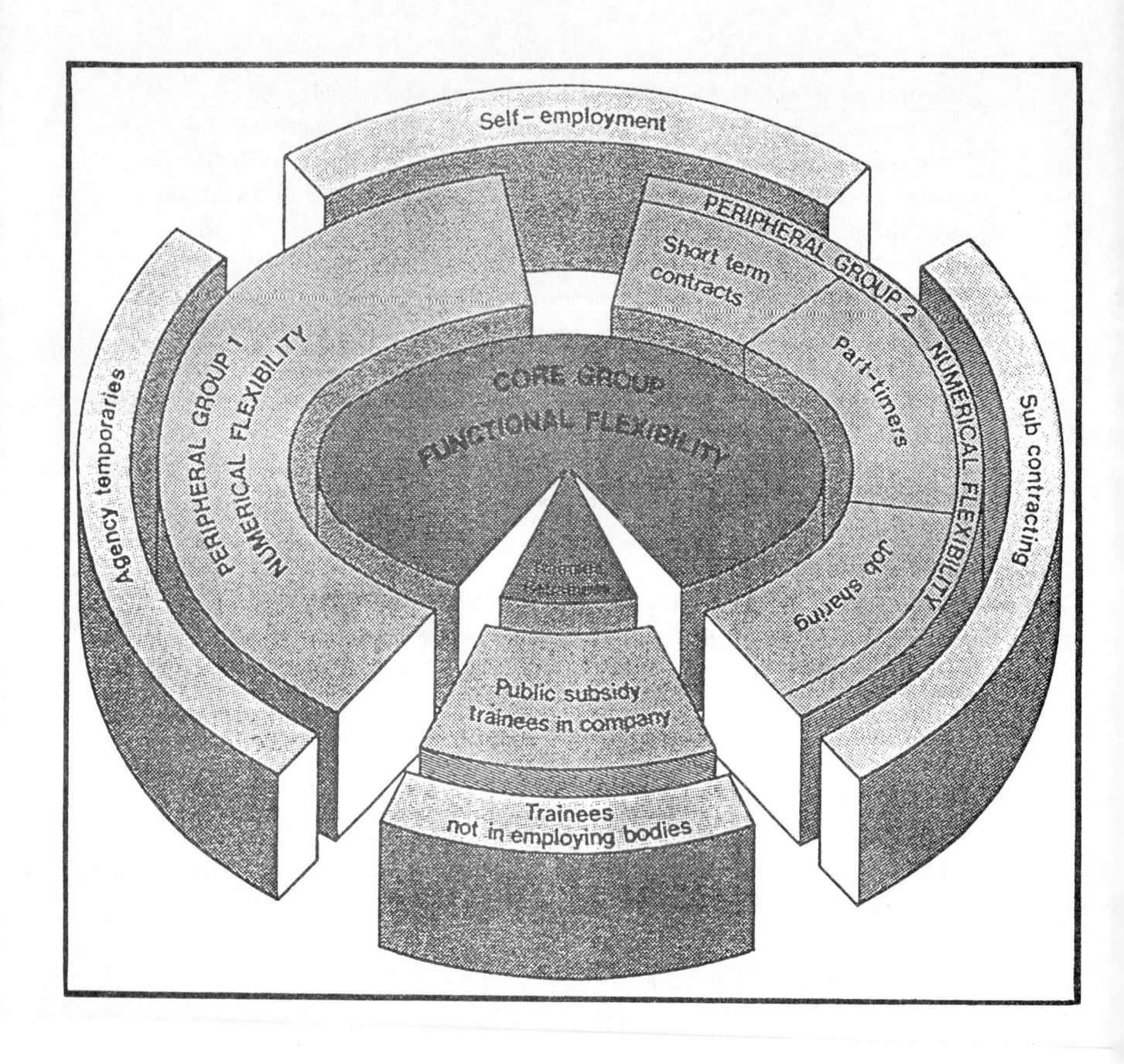

One of the basic questions raised by this diagram concerns the
existence or non-existence of bridges between the various groups.
Some workers are doubtless doomed to be forever peripheral workers,
while core workers are relatively protected.

This diagram is certainly a good illustration of a trend, but it is difficult to know how many firms have put such a policy into action.

In stressing the risks of flexibility, J.M. Maury did not mention this duality of flexibility. He referred explicitly to the fact that a firm's only option is numerical flexibility, which is in the short term the easiest route, if not the most effective.

The model presented by Atkinson is in fact a synthesis, a sort of "ideal type" in the Weberian sense, which enables us to understand a situation without necessarily being a faithful reflection of it.

Robert Boyer's thesis is fairly similar to the one just mentioned, but Boyer further refines the categories used by Atkinson in that he sees five possible facets to flexibility.

The first is connected with "the varying degree of adaptability of production organization". This adaptability depends to a large extent on technological and organizational options: it evokes, if we have correctly understood the author, the "flexible workshop", ie the fully automated workshop.

The second meaning of flexibility concerns the ability of workers to change jobs within a given, or possibly a rapidly changing, organizational structure. For this, the workforce needs to be multi-skilled: "ability to fill varied posts, adequately broad general and technical training, involvement of workers in quality control, absence of insurmountable barriers between workers, foremen and engineers. The symbol of this new direction in industrial labour is nothing more than a modern version of the Proudhonian worker". This echoes Atkinson's functional flexibility.

"According to a third definition, flexibility measures itself against the weakness of the legal constraints governing employment contracts and, in particular, dismissals. By contrast with the preceding senses, this definition places the emphasis on the institutional aspects relating to labour law or to collective agreement clauses...

The ideal type appears to be an employment contract whose conditions can be altered from one day to the next. This flexibility would ideally be achieved by extending the intermediate wage-earners to the whole of society." This flexibility is similar to the numerical flexibility described by Atkinson.

Flexibility, still according to Robert Boyer, may have a fourth meaning and "indicate the sensitivity of wages (whether nominal or real) to the financial situation of each firm or the general economic situation affecting the labour market". The extent of unemployment would be explained by the rigidity of opposition to any drop in wages. Or, "insensitivity of wage levels to the deterioration in the terms of trade, the stagnation of productivity and the spread of unemployment encourage a delayed and inflationary adjustment which then makes austerity policies necessary". This conception of flexibility bases the development of competition on the labour market, the individualization of wages and a relaxation or abolition of legislation on minimum wages. For Boyer, "the logic of this flexibility is nothing more than a form of payment by results".

This flexibility may come into conflict with the preceding type in that it theoretically allows employment to be guaranteed provided that it is accompanied by very large wage fluctuations, in contrast with the maintenance of high wages, which implies recourse to temporary, and sometimes long-term, unemployment.

Finally, the fifth and final definition of flexibility is "understood as the possibility for some firms of avoiding some of their social security and tax contributions and, more generally, freeing themselves of the government regulations which limit their freedom of management."

The aim is to reduce the gap between the net income received by employees and its overall cost for the firm. "The symbol of this type of flexibility may be either the black economy on the Italian model or a return to the minimal state so dear to the proponents of liberalism or, and this is certainly the most likely scenario, a two-tier labour force as regards means of access to social insurance and observance of labour law".

This analysis of research on "flexibility in Europe" has been described because it bears directly on our subject, but a much wider-ranging thesis covers variations in the macroeconomic parameters that characterize adjustments of employment to developments in the production system.

Between description and prediction, the question which is raised is "where do we go from here"? Because of its extent and the dramas that go with it, unemployment is quite rightly demanding all the attention and makes a more forward-looking vision difficult.

The theories which have been explained here help to clarify what is happening within firms.

The theories could be contested on the basis of narrowly interpreted quantitative data. There is room to believe that the Atkinson diagram reflects the situation in only a very limited number of firms and that the vision of Boyer (or of M. Piore) is too eschatological by far. Yet has not the role of researchers always been to draw attention to the risks?

Part 2: Opinions

As we have seen in earlier sections, the studies and research on flexibility (or at least on the aspect of flexibility constituted by new forms of work) concentrate on describing its underlying logic and its possible or confirmed consequences. As a general rule, when they are not purely theoretical research papers, these publications base their discourse on observed behaviour patterns. Temporary jobs and part-time working are on the increase, etc. But what are the opinions of those who are most directly affected?

Ambiguities of opinion on new forms of work

Surveys on this subject have been conducted increasingly in the various European countries, although not on the scale of significance of opinion polls in the sphere of, say, consumption or of political views.

The reason is that these surveys on new forms of work present considerable difficulties as regards their drafting and interpretation, and it is usually practically impossible to compare them.

The difficulties are primarily connected with the field to be explored, which, as we have seen, is particularly complex. Wage-earners in the developed industrial countries are increasingly aware of this complexity and consequently hold fairly subtle and varying opinions depending on whether it is their own case or a general measure that is in question. For a universe as vast as that represented by the world of work, we have little idea of how opinions are structured or how they develop. These theoretical difficulties have the practical effect of making any survey on this subject extremely laborious since, in order for the field to be fully covered, they must necessarily be based on a very extensive questionnaire.

This explains why, for each country, there are effectively numerous partial surveys covering a limited aspect of flexibility, usually the organization of working time.

These surveys may be of descriptive interest but they are far from having the predictive interest of opinion polls on political attitudes.

Here we are actually touching on another problem associated with these surveys and their comparability. In the highly complex domain of work, where judgements and opinions are based on very subtle arbitrations and comparisons, there may be very wide discrepancies between opinion and behaviour.

An interesting example is provided by the surveys conducted among employers on what they currently see as constraints on recruitment, which may be another way of viewing flexibility.

A survey commissioned by the CNPF in France and conducted among a representative sample of employers revealed that the real or presumed difficulty of dismissing staff was a considerable obstacle to recruitment (Pragma, 1984). In view of the findings of this survey, employers' associations naturally applied pressure to achieve the abolition of government authorization for dismissals in order to free employers from measures that they saw as a real handicap in adapting their firms to cope with market constraints. The relaxation of constraints finally approved by the French Government has however not resulted in the behavioural patterns that might normally have been expected on the basis of the opinions expressed. It is now much easier to dismiss staff but this has not led to any increase in recruitment.

How should such a discrepancy be interpreted? One explanation that can be immediately discounted is the highly polemical supposition that the discrepancy between opinions expressed and actual behaviour can be put down to fickleness and irresponsibility. The majority of French employers - and they are not the only ones, if we are to believe certain European surveys - believed in all good faith that government authorization of dismissals was a real and major obstacle to recruitment. This opinion may well have been based essentially on an ideological view of the situation, but what is new about that? This phenomenon can doubtless be explained by using certain elements of the theory of requirements. The satisfaction of certain requirements does not necessarily lead to action. That satisfaction is not a motivating force. Thus, the abolition of government authorization of dismissals is probably in part more of a psychological obstacle than a real and objective one but, whatever its nature, it is still of considerable significance.

This example illustrates the limitations of, and difficulties in interpreting, these surveys. It is important to realize that this kind of government measure is generally considered by employers to be a nuisance, but it is very risky to assume that its abolition will ipso facto lead to the creation of some 400 000 jobs.

On the other hand, the existence of such a highly structured pattern of opinion focused on a specific point often means that it will be very difficult to convince its exponents of the need to broaden the scope of their diagnosis and look further for the causes of company inflexibility.

It is in fact essential to have a better knowledge of the opinions of both employers and employees, not in order to deduce from them the actual situation but rather to identify the obstacles that will be faced in the implementation of certain measures and, where applicable, to consider the actions to be taken to alter these opinions.

The numerous surveys and studies conducted in the various countries enable us to perceive relatively accurately, at national level, existing opinions on the current major themes of flexibility. Nonetheless, and because they were not designed with this in view, these investigations do not lend themselves well to comparative studies. This is why we decided to concentrate on European surveys which allow immediate comparisons on similar bases.

I. Surveys among workers

The most recent survey on flexibility was conducted in the spring of 1985 in the then 10 Member States of the European Community, and in Spain and Portugal in early 1986.

Overall, 12 000 people were questioned, ie a representative sample of 1000 people per country. Questionnaires were completed during personal interviews and not by post, and all the questions were close-ended.

The personal details recorded were: sex, age, income, function (manual worker, white-collar/office worker, executive/top management), union membership (active member, only paying member, not member but sympathetic, not member and not interested), weekly working time (hours), sector (public or private) and country.

These details are interesting but are lacking on at least two essential points: the size of the firm in which the employee works and its distance from his home. Commuting time is one of the major factors taken into account by employees in assessing the advantages and disadvantages of any reorganization, and particularly a reduction, of their working time. Relatively few questions were asked but they all concentrated on the traditional aspects of flexibility: length and organization of working time, the bond of solidarity likely to exist between employees and their firm, profit-sharing and the individualization of pay.

It should finally be added that this questionnaire was also presented to a representative sample of unemployed persons and students aged 16-24.

Before looking in more detail at the responses to the various questions posed in this survey, we should point to the most significant finding - the existence of a Community-wide opinion.

Despite the diversity of economic situations, of cultures and, more simply, of legal regulations governing working life in the various Member States, the questions put to them have a meaning, and an almost identical meaning, for all the respondents, from Spain to Denmark (as is indicated by the very low rate of "don't knows" and "no answers"). This finding had already been suggested by the very large European survey of values conducted in the early 1980s under the direction of Jean Stoetzel and applied to a representative sample: "there is no radical difference of opinions between the various European nationals, any more than between different age groups and social groupings or between holders of divergent political or religious views. Not only is there no radical difference, there is very considerable proximity, arising no doubt from the fact that they belong to the same civilization. Yet this similarity of views does not imply sameness, and marked nuances give each country its own individual character and express its identity".

This is a very fundamental point as this "proximity", this existence of Community-wide opinions, gives cause for optimism about the possibility of introducing regulations on the broadest level.

a) Money rather than time

European opinion on this subject has changed since the end of the 1970s, though we have to interpret this change with some caution.

The information available, and particularly the Eurobarometer survey of October/November 1977, allows a comparison of responses on the basis of workers' position in the income pyramid, as is indicated by the diagram on the following page.

Preference for higher pay or shorter working time (European Community)

(Breakdown of responses according to position in the income pyramid)

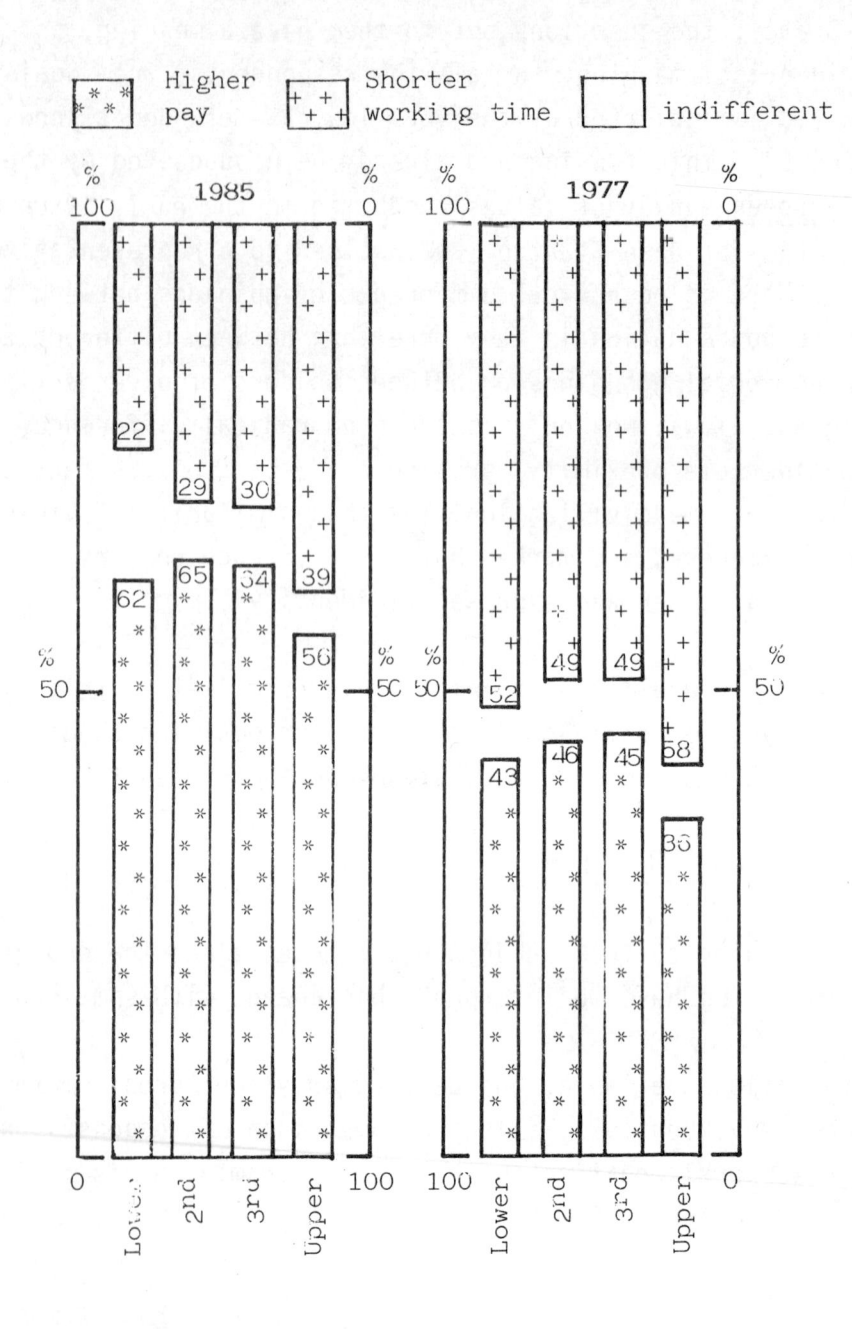

| ✻ ✻ | Higher pay | + + | Shorter working time | ☐ | indifferent |

1985

Quartile	Higher pay	Shorter working time
Lower	62	22
2nd	65	29
3rd	54	30
Upper	56	39

1977

Quartile	Higher pay	Shorter working time
Lower	43	52
2nd	46	49
3rd	45	49
Upper	58	35

Quartiles of the income pyramid

Source: EEC employee survey, Spring 1985 and Eurobarometer, October/November 1977.

The economic crisis which is affecting the European countries, albeit to varying degrees, has helped to bring about a profound change in attitudes. In 1977, more than half of the respondents would have preferred to see a reduction in their working time rather than a rise in their pay and this trend was confirmed by the survey of "current values". In 1980, more than half (57%) of Europeans would have liked work to occupy a smaller place in their lives, but 94% were mainly in favour of a simpler and more natural way of life, with more time to devote to their families and their personal development. These "values" are the reflection of a period of strong growth. The present crisis is forcing people to be more realistic, but there are still very strong traces of this heady dream of a more convivial way of life.

Today, 62% of the European employees questioned would, if they had the choice, prefer an increase in pay to a reduction in working hours (1). Yet still no fewer than a third (30%) of them would prefer the opposite, as the diagram on the following page indicates (see detailed results in the Annex).

The results do however vary very considerably between the various Member States, depending both on income trends over the past few years and on standards of living: nearly 80% of Portuguese and Irish workers would prefer an increase in pay, whereas the Dutch, and particularly the Danish, would opt for more free time.

---

(1) The question asked was:
 If the choice were offered at the next wage round, which of the following possibilities would you prefer?
 1. Increase in pay for the same hours of work as now
 2. No increase in pay but shorter working time
 3. Don't know

Choice between increase in pay or reduction in working hours

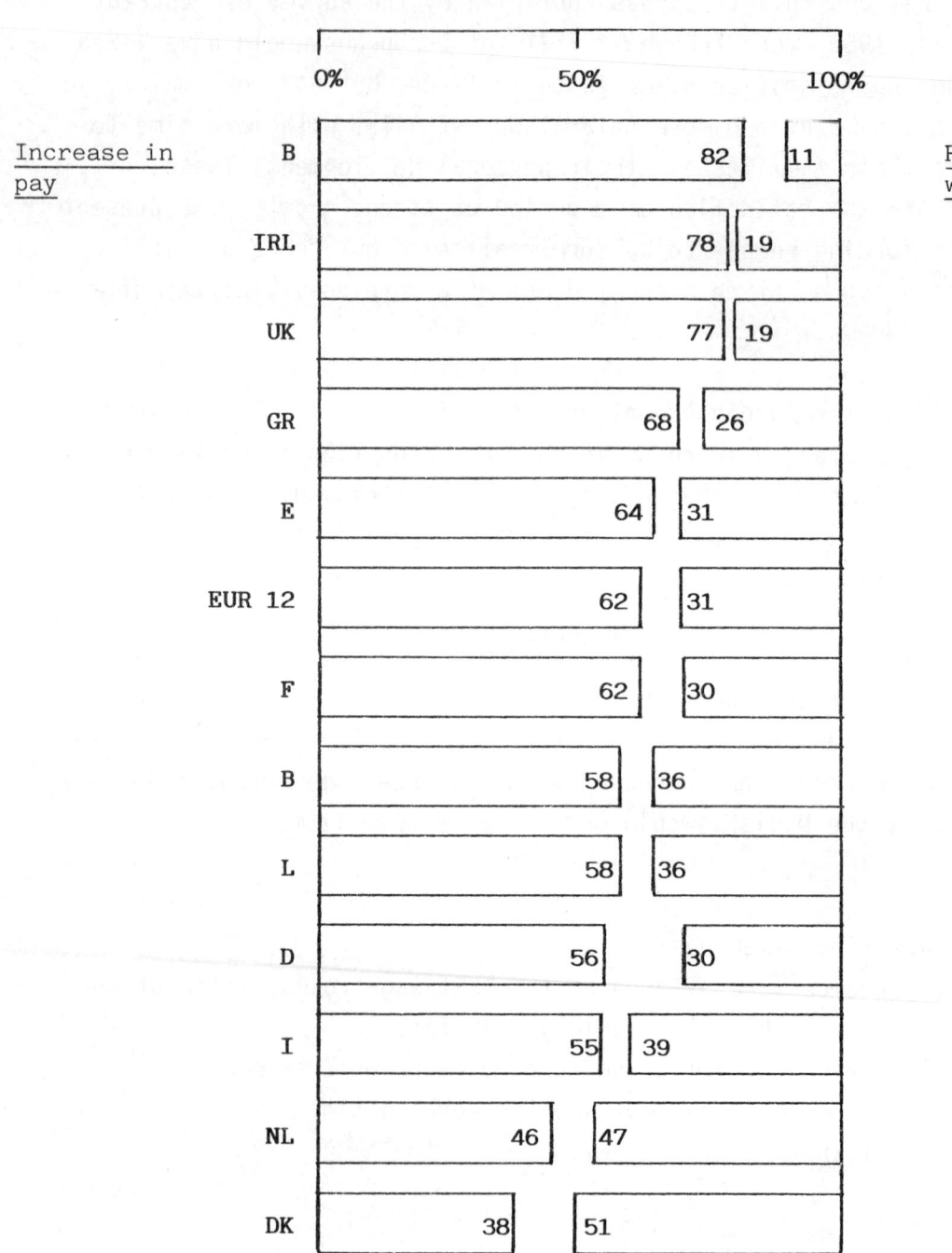

	Increase in pay	Reduction in working hours
B	82	11
IRL	78	19
UK	77	19
GR	68	26
E	64	31
EUR 12	62	31
F	62	30
B	58	36
L	58	36
D	56	30
I	55	39
NL	46	47
DK	38	51

The sex of workers and whether they work in the private or public sector are not deciding variables as regards this question. Part-time workers are less in favour than "normal" employees of a reduction in working hours (24% as against 37%), which is to be expected. On the other hand, it is people with the longest working hours who are least desirous of a reduction in working time.

This finding is only apparently paradoxical. It reveals a very significant problem which has often been identified by researchers in the various European countries - the correlation between working hours and job satisfaction. This may well be a very curt equation but it is not without reason that those with varied and interesting jobs "weren't clock-watchers."

It is in fact very difficult to "enrich" people's working lives by simply reducing the hours they work. By the same token, extensive recourse to half-time working or reduced hours is very often indicative of low-skilled work which offers little job satisfaction.

This question regarding pay and working hours was complemented by a second question to allow a comparison between workers' present working hours and what they see as the ideal working time (1).

More than half (57%) of those questioned were entirely satisfied with their working hours; 7% would like to work more and 36% less. The ideal number of working hours is in fact fairly close to present working hours, with a preference for a reduction. Thus, 3.8% of

---

(1) The question asked was:
1. What is your present working time per week?
2. You sometimes hear that not everyone is fully satisfied with his/her current working time. Assuming that the present hourly wage rate remained unchanged, how many hours per week would you like to work?

employees work between 30 and 34 hours a week and 17.5% would like to do so. A quarter of full-time workers (working at least 35 hours a week) would like to see a reduction in their working hours, even if it had to involve a drop in their wages. Men, with very few exceptions, are against the idea of half-time working. This is also the case, however, for women with full-time jobs, as only one in ten of them would like to work half-time. Here too, opinion confirms research findings. Half-time working is preferred by women with heavy family commitments, but this does not represent a real personal preference. This is not contradictory to the fact that part-time workers are satisfied with their working hours. A quarter of those working less than 20 hours a week would like to work longer hours and 12% would like to work full-time (see detailed results in the Annex).

To sum up these two questions, it could be said that, even though the desire to see working hours reduced is much weaker than it was in 1977, nearly a third of workers still fervently wish for a reduction in their working time, since they would go so far as to accept a stagnation or even a fall in their incomes. That represents a fairly high demand; the question is whether the supply is available from firms.

b) Flexibility rather than rigidity

Two questions aimed to assess employees' opinions on monthly or annual variations in working times and on new ways of organizing working time, particularly weekend working.

The responses to the first question (1) are quite interesting and are obviously based on prevailing ideas.

Fewer than 40% of employees want no change, but just as few are in favour of variations in working hours being negotiated to meet production or work organization requirements, with only 16% being in favour of an annual organization of working time. Men's and women's responses to this question are almost identical; by contrast, and quite understandably, it is workers over the age of 55 who are the most attached to the idea of regular daily working hours. Union membership leads to an above-average inclination towards flexibility. It is people who work the longest hours (41 hours a week and more) who are by far the most in favour of a monthly or annual flexibility of working time, whilst half-time workers are the most "rigid": some 4% of employees working more than 41 hours a week are in favour of monthly flexibility and 25% (the highest figure) are in favour of annual flexibility. In contrast to prevailing beliefs, public-sector workers are more in favour of flexible working hours than private-sector workers are.

Finally, the widest distinctions observed were between the various Member States, as the diagram on the following page indicates.

---

(1) The question asked was:
Let us assume that more flexible working-time arrangements will be offered in the near future. Which one would you prefer, assuming that the salary is the same?
1. Same working hours every day.
2. Fixed amount of working hours per month but the number of working days and working hours per day could be agreed according to production and/or work organization requirements.
3. Fixed amount of working hours per year but with periods of hard work which would involve long hours and other periods of shorter hours or holidays according to production and/or work organization requirements.

New working time arrangements

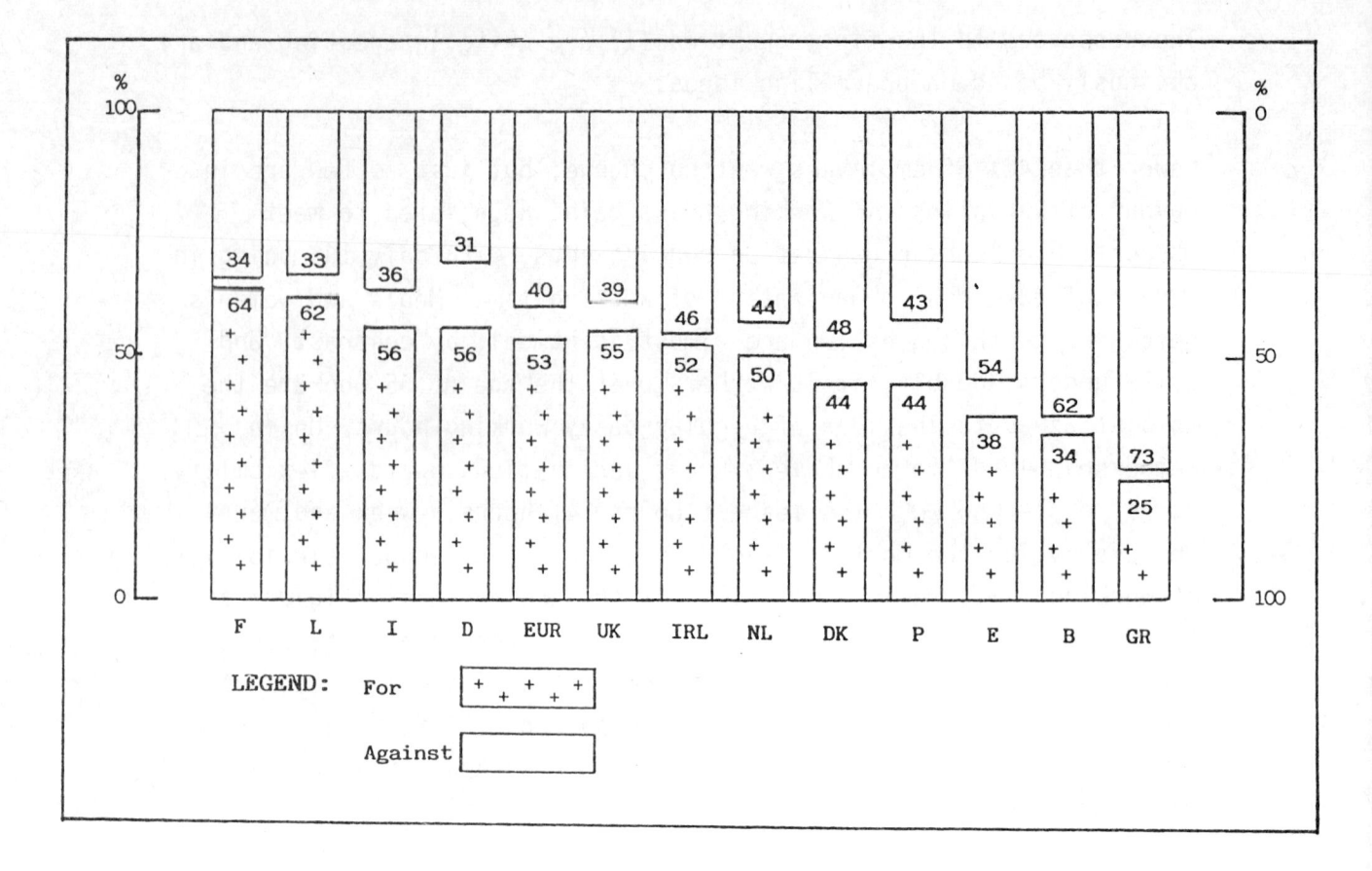

	F	L	I	D	EUR	UK	IRL	NL	DK	P	E	B	GR
Against	34	33	36	31	40	39	46	44	48	43	54	62	73
For	64	62	56	56	53	55	52	50	44	44	38	34	25

LEGEND: For `+ + +` Against ` `

The French easily come top of the league of the most "flexible" workers, followed by workers in Luxembourg, Italy and Germany, while Greek, Belgian and Spanish workers are the most "rigid" in this respect.

The question which complements this one is harder to interpret, partly because of the way in which it is worded (1); the large number of "no answers" and "indifferents" confirms this. The percentage of

---

(1) Supposing you were offered the following working time arrangements:
You work for example one Saturday a month, or else you work five times a month up to 22.00 hrs in the evening, and as a counterpart, your working time per year is reduced by 5% (that could be 2 hours less work per week in the average or else it could be two weeks more holiday a year).

workers very much in favour of this suggestion never rises above 14%
(see detailed results in the Annex). Yet if we add to this percentage
those people who are rather in favour, we find that just over a third
of workers are ready to accept this kind of flexibility.

Cross-referenced analysis of these two questions shows that those who
are in favour of a monthly arrangement of working time are not
necessarily in favour of working until 22.00 hrs in the evening or on
Saturdays. By contrast, a quarter of those who prefer to work the
same number of hours every week are not against evening and weekend
work which would be compensated by extra holidays. Supplementary
research would be needed here to explain the contrast between these
opinions, which can no doubt be put down to constraints outside work.

c) <u>Solidarity, despite everything</u>

Half of the employees questioned think that a drop in wages when
their company is in difficulty is acceptable, provided of course that
they get a share of the profits when the situation improves (1). A
third of employees are against this idea. Women are more in favour of
it than men are (54% as against 49%) and young workers more than
older workers (55% as against 42%). People on the lowest and highest
incomes have very similar opinions here and hold a very favourable
view of this suggestion. This may be explained, in the case of those

---

(1) The question here was:
    In some countries, people are accepting lower salaries when their
    company is in difficulty, with the understanding that they will
    get a share of the profits when the company is doing better.
    What is your personal opinion of such an arrangement?
    Are you 1. very much in favour
             2. rather in favour
             3. rather against
             4. very much against
             5. indifferent
             6. don't know

on the lowest wages, by the feeling that it would be better to make a temporary sacrifice than end up on the dole, whilst a temporary drop in salary would pose few problems for those on the highest incomes. It is also true that the largest number of 'indifferents" or "don't knows" occurs in the lower quartile group (see tables in the Annex). The other variables are not very decisive here, but there are strong differences in the majority opinion between the various Member States: the numbers of workers in favour in the Netherlands, France and Ireland are way above the European average, while the Belgians are the most hostile to the idea of a temporary sacrifice. The Germans and Belgians are the least in favour, and the Germans are also very indecisive as regards this suggestion.

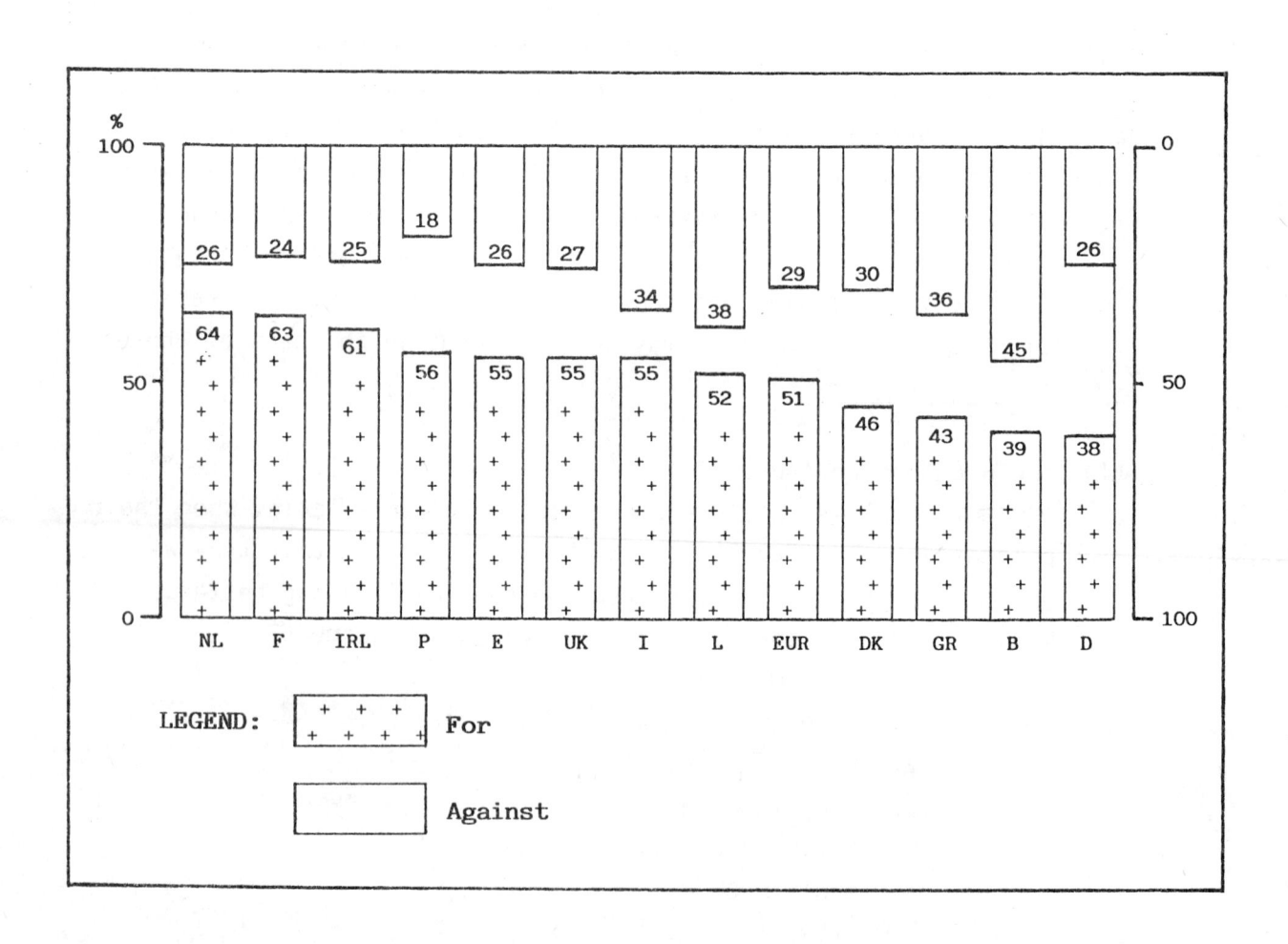

Country	For	Against
NL	64	26
F	63	24
IRL	61	25
P	56	18
E	55	26
UK	55	27
I	55	34
L	52	38
EUR	51	29
DK	46	30
GR	43	36
B	39	45
D	38	26

LEGEND: + For / Against

This attitude is easier to understand when one realizes how uncommon profit-sharing is, in whatever form, in the various European countries (see table in the Annex).

d)   But "vive la différence"

The "equal pay for equal work" slogan is no longer a vote-winner as it meets the approval of only a quarter of European workers, whereas more than half (56%) of them think that, irrespective of the post occupied, pay should be based on personal merit. This is not a wish but a confirmed fact. Only 16% of European workers questioned thought that pay differentials accurately reflected differences in individual performance and a quarter thought they were more or less sufficient, though the same proportion considered them to be insufficient. What is particularly interesting in the responses to the questions asked here is the very large measure of agreement, whatever the socio-demographic or socio-economic variables. Union membership or sympathy was not decisive here. Suprisingly enough, the sector in which respondents were employed did affect their answers, and not in the way one might have expected: in the private sector, 44% of employees thought that pay differentials were sufficient and 30% thought they were insufficient; the responses in the public sector were less favourable (33% sufficient; 38% insufficient).

Here too, however, the differences between countries were fairly marked: 38% of French respondents thought that pay differentials were insufficient, whereas the Danish, Belgian and Irish respondents were generally satisfied with the differentials, such as they are.

For or against pay differentials based on individual performance

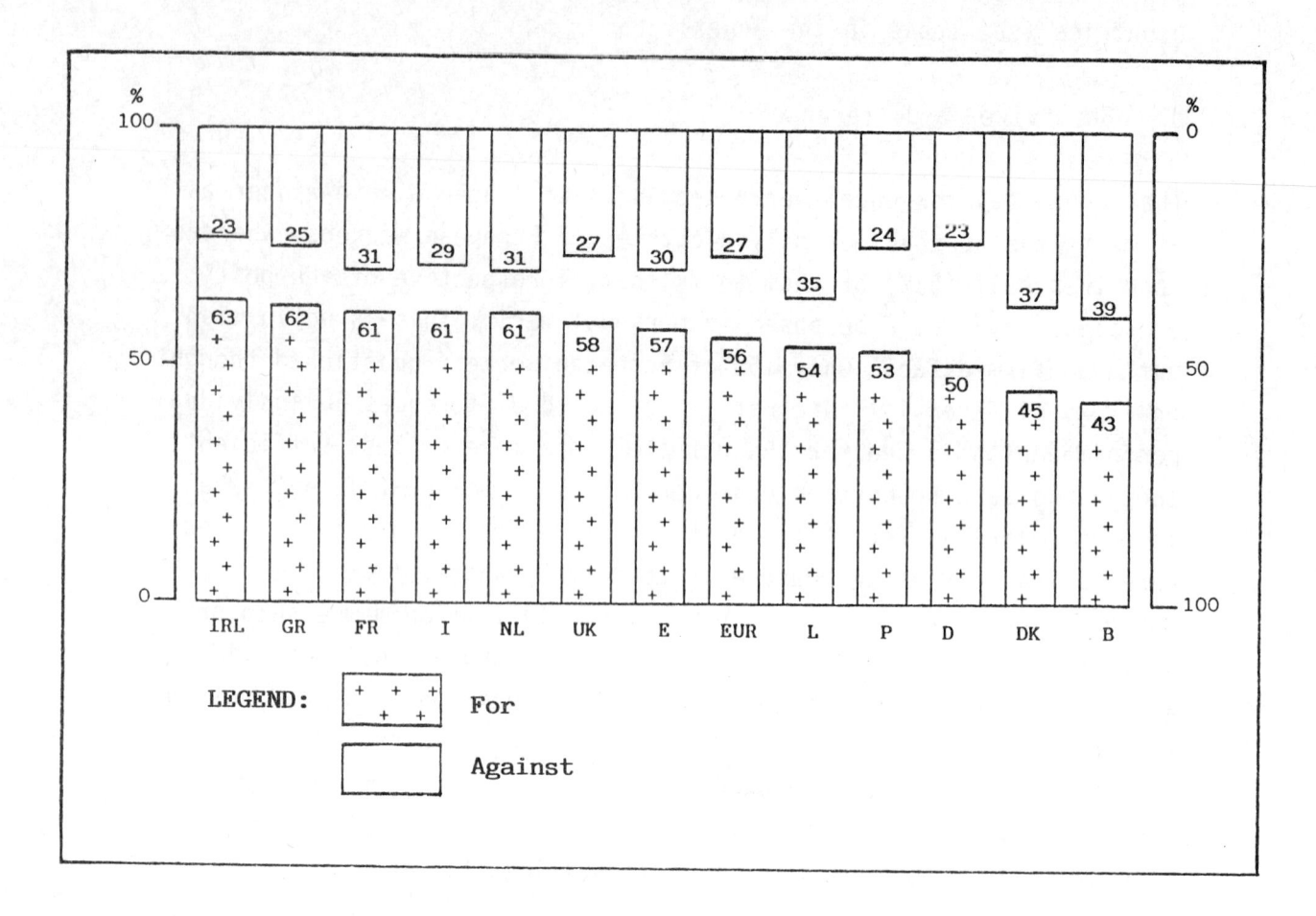

	IRL	GR	FR	I	NL	UK	E	EUR	L	P	D	DK	B
Against	23	25	31	29	31	27	30	27	35	24	23	37	39
For	63	62	61	61	61	58	57	56	54	53	50	45	43

LEGEND: + For / □ Against

The questionnaire whose main results have just been described here was also presented to unemployed persons and to young people aged 16-24 who had never worked. In general, their responses differ little from those given by workers.

The unemployed differ from those in work in their acceptance of the idea of working unsociable hours or days (ie Saturday or evening working).

Young people who have never worked differ from young workers of the same age in their wish for flexibility in working time arrangements.

Overall, this questionnaire shows that European workers are more "flexible" than they are claimed to be, are more attached to their company than one might think and do not quite match the national stereotypes usually applied to them.

On some issues, the national attitudes seem far enough apart to suggest that, in order to be effective, any supra-national "regulations" will have to take account of these differences.

II. The opinions of employers

If it is difficult to grasp workers' opinions on such a vast and controversial subject as flexibility, it is certainly an even more complex task to understand the opinions of employers. A survey of a representative sample can cover only a limited number of simple questions.

In conjunction with the employee survey, the Commission of the European Communities asked the national economic institutes (responsible for conducting the monthly Community survey of firms) to gauge employers' opinions on "obstacles to recruitment". The survey was conducted in industry and commerce in December 1985 and February 1986 respectively. All the Member States, with the exception of Denmark, Portugal and Spain, took part in the survey conducted in industry. In the commerce and distribution sector, the survey was conducted in only five of the Member States: Belgium, France, Germany, the Netherlands and the UK.

1. Manufacturing industry

a) Background

. Fairly pessimistic outlook

Before examining employers' opinions of the specific situation of their firms, it is certainly of interest to look at their more general opinions on past and future trends as regards employment in general.

For the 12 months preceding the survey, 42% thought that the trend at European level was down and 32% thought that it was up. Yet there are very sharp contrasts between the Member States. Italy and France were the most pessimistic, while Germany, Belgium and the Netherlands had a more optimistic view of the past year. The future (ie 1986) was expected to be an attenuated projection of the past. Some 40% of employers thought there would in fact be no change, 37% were pessimistic and only 21% had an optimistic outlook. Here too, there are marked differences between countries. The pessimists (Italy and France) were even more pessimistic than they had been, and the optimists were looking towards stabilization rather than any real improvement. The diagrams on the following page illustrate the answers to these two questions.

Employment trends

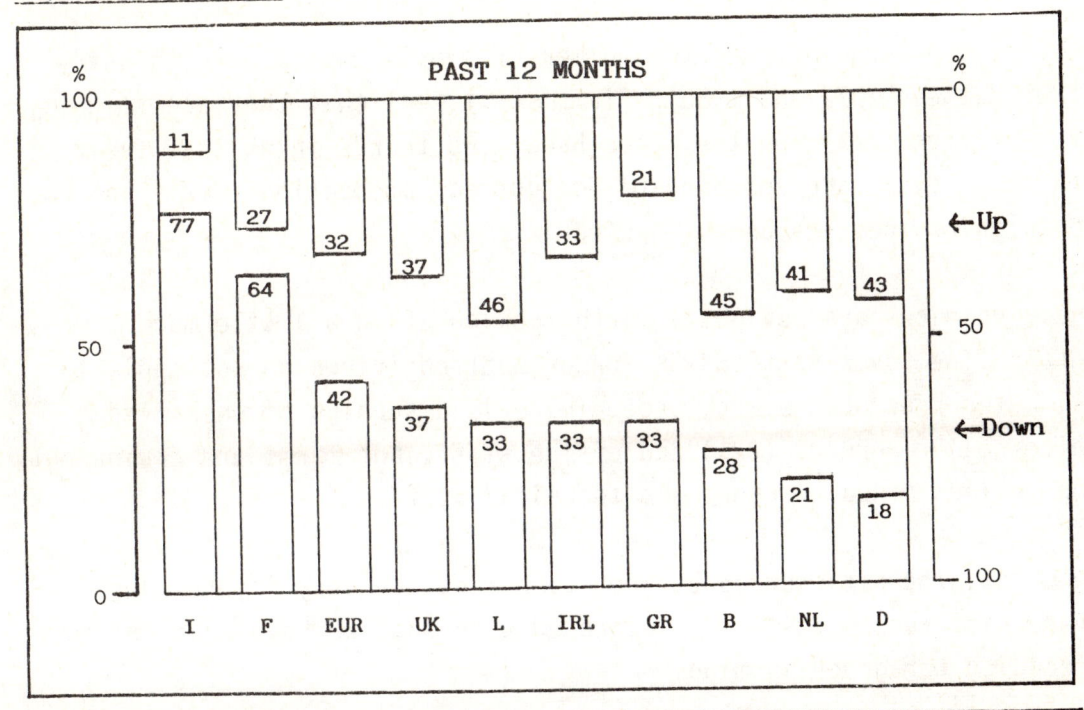

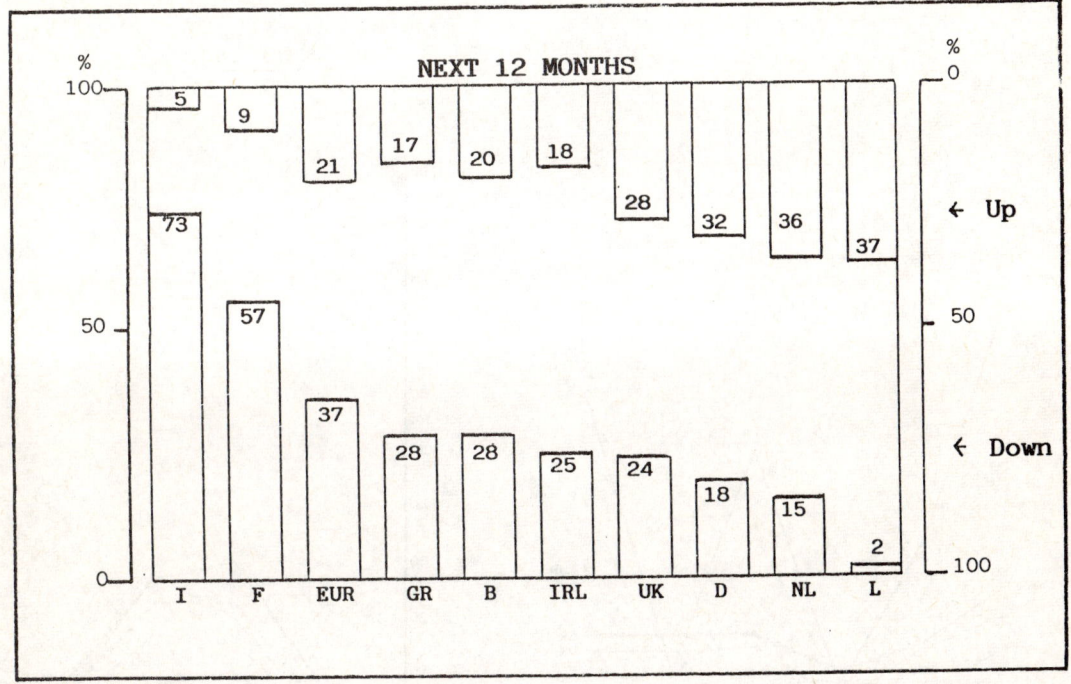

PAST 12 MONTHS

	I	F	EUR	UK	L	IRL	GR	B	NL	D
Up	11	27	32	37	—	33	21	—	41	43
(mid)	77	64	—	—	46	—	—	45	—	—
Down	—	—	42	37	33	33	33	28	21	18

NEXT 12 MONTHS

	I	F	EUR	GR	B	IRL	UK	D	NL	L
Up	5	9	21	17	20	18	28	32	36	37
(mid)	73	57	37	—	—	—	—	—	—	—
Down	—	—	—	28	28	25	24	18	15	2

The figures we have on employment show that the employers' opinion as regards these trends is fairly precise and well-founded.

Too many unskilled workers, too few skilled workers

Despite the large drop in the number of people employed in industry (-20% between 1972 and 1985), firms still feel that they are slightly over-staffed (27%). On the other hand, two thirds think that their staffing levels are appropriate for current production levels and one tenth think they are under-staffed.

These opinions are obviously worth looking at in a little more detail. The "over-staffed" or "under-staffed" views do not apply to all categories of the workforce. There is a surplus of unskilled white-collar workers (32%) and office staff, but firms are crying out for skilled manual workers and technical staff.

Here too, the differences between countries are very interesting. These differences must be interpreted with what we have said in the preceding paragraph in mind.

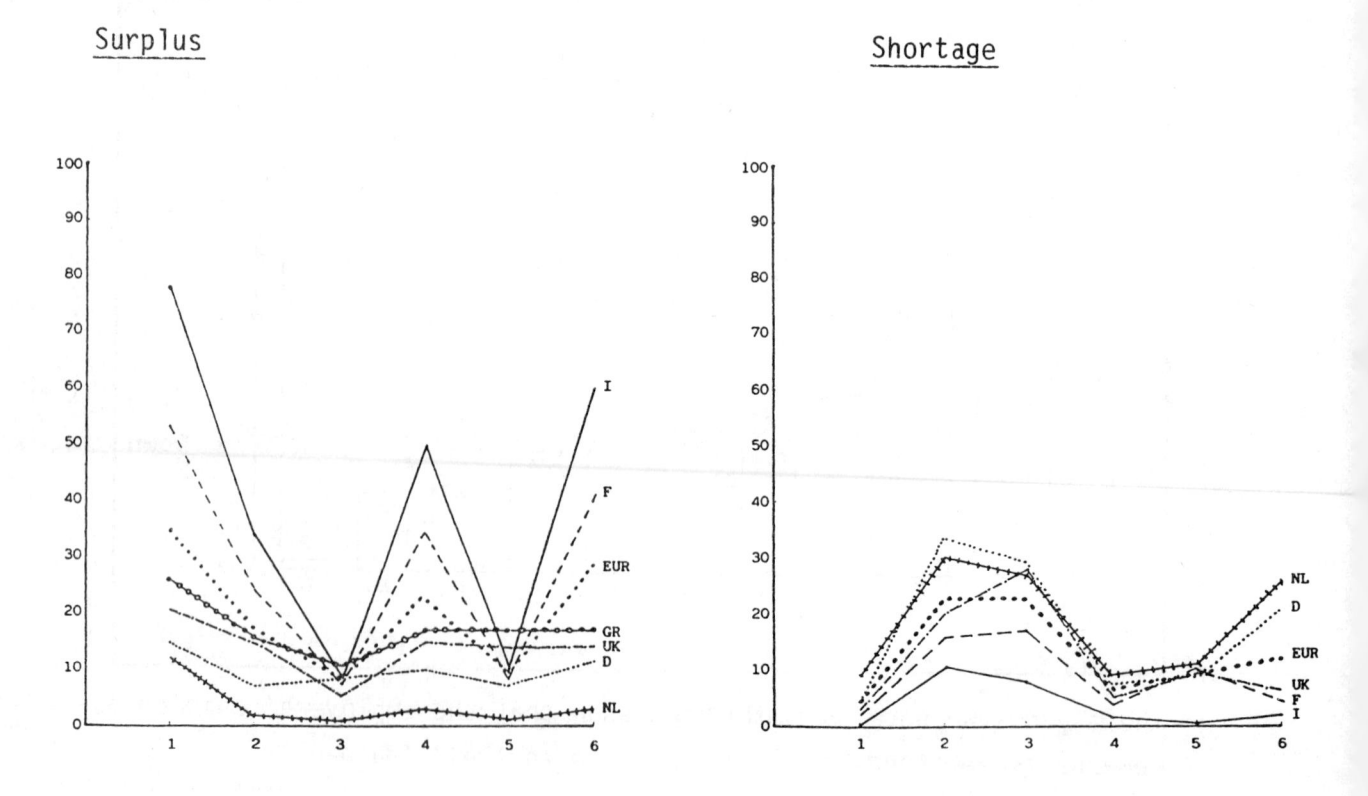

Surplus   Shortage

1. Unskilled manual   4. Office/sales staff
2. Skilled manual   5. Management
3. Technicians   6. Total

Italy and France have very specific problems, as the graphs on the previous page show. The opinion curve varies widely according to the category of the workforce in question. In both countries, employers are complaining mainly of a surplus of unskilled manual workers and white-collar workers, whereas the surpluses in Germany, the UK and the Netherlands are fairly evenly distributed.

The Netherlands and Germany contrast with Italy and France in that they both have similar surpluses in just about every category of the workforce.

In all cases, the feeling is that there are too many unskilled manual and white-collar workers (do these opinions reflect, among other things, technological change?).

Labour shortages contrast with the surpluses. Curiously, but only apparently paradoxically, it is those countries which use the highest percentages of skilled manual labour which are suffering the greatest shortfalls. Skilled manual workers and technical staff seem to be in short supply throughout Europe, but particularly in the Netherlands and Germany. Unskilled manual workers, white-collar workers and also management staff seem to be in adequate supply and even where shortages do exist, they are much less serious than the shortage of technical staff.

The fairly pessimistic view of the future and this general and specific surplus of labour enables us to visualize the context in which opinions concerned more directly with flexibility are expressed.

b) <u>Obstacles to recruitment: the reasons given</u>

The following diagram indicates the main reasons for which European manufacturing firms feel they cannot increase their staffing levels.

Obstacles to increasing employment in the manufacturing industry

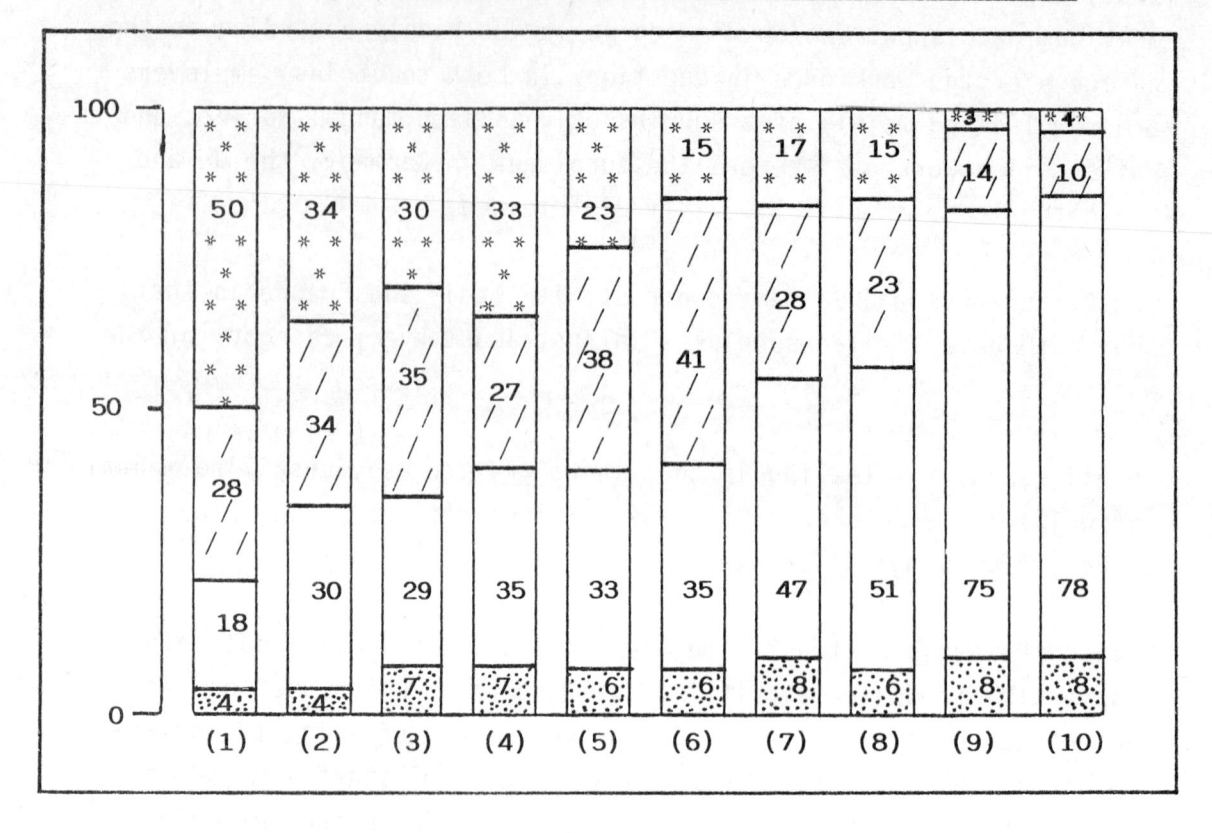

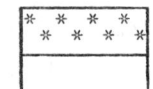

	(1)	(2)	(3)	(4)	(5)	(6)	(7)	(8)	(9)	(10)
Very important	50	34	30	33	23	15	17	15	3	4
									14	10
Important	28	34	35	27	38	41	28	23	—	—
Not important	18	30	29	35	33	35	47	51	75	78
No answer	4	4	7	7	6	6	8	6	8	8

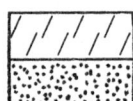

Legend:
- ✱ ✱ ✱ ✱ Very important
- ///// Important
- ▭ Not important
- ░░░ No answer

Legend
1. Insufficient and uncertain demand
2. Insufficient profit margin due to product prices
3. Insufficient profit margin due to non-wage labour costs
4. Insufficient flexibility in regulations governing recruitment and dismissal
5. Rationalization and/or introduction of new technology
6. Insufficient profit margin due to wage levels
7. Insufficient profit margin due to other than labour costs
8. Shortage of adequately skilled applicants
9. Increase in contracting out
10. Insufficient production capacity

Certainly the most important point for all firms is the insufficient level of demand, followed by strong competition, which forces them to adopt very stringent pricing policies. The two major reasons given, then, are connected with the market. These are followed, with almost equal importance, by non-wage labour costs, insufficient flexibility in recruitment and dismissal regulations, modernization of organization methods and equipment, and wage levels.

The reasons mentioned next are of decreasing importance, to the point where they have almost no impact at all. Firms' production capacities do not really count at all, contracting out is not an obstacle to recruitment, at least not in the eyes of employers, and the shortage of skilled workers, though it does count for something in a third of cases, is not a decisive factor in impeding recruitment.

These very general results need to be broken down according to the size of firms and the country concerned.

This survey has been used by the Institut National de la Statistique et des Etudes Economiques (National Institute for Statistics and Economic Studies) in France to compile a detailed study of the situation in France, Belgium and the UK (Elbaum, 1987). The diagram on the following page has been drawn from this study.

Reasons given for not increasing employment *

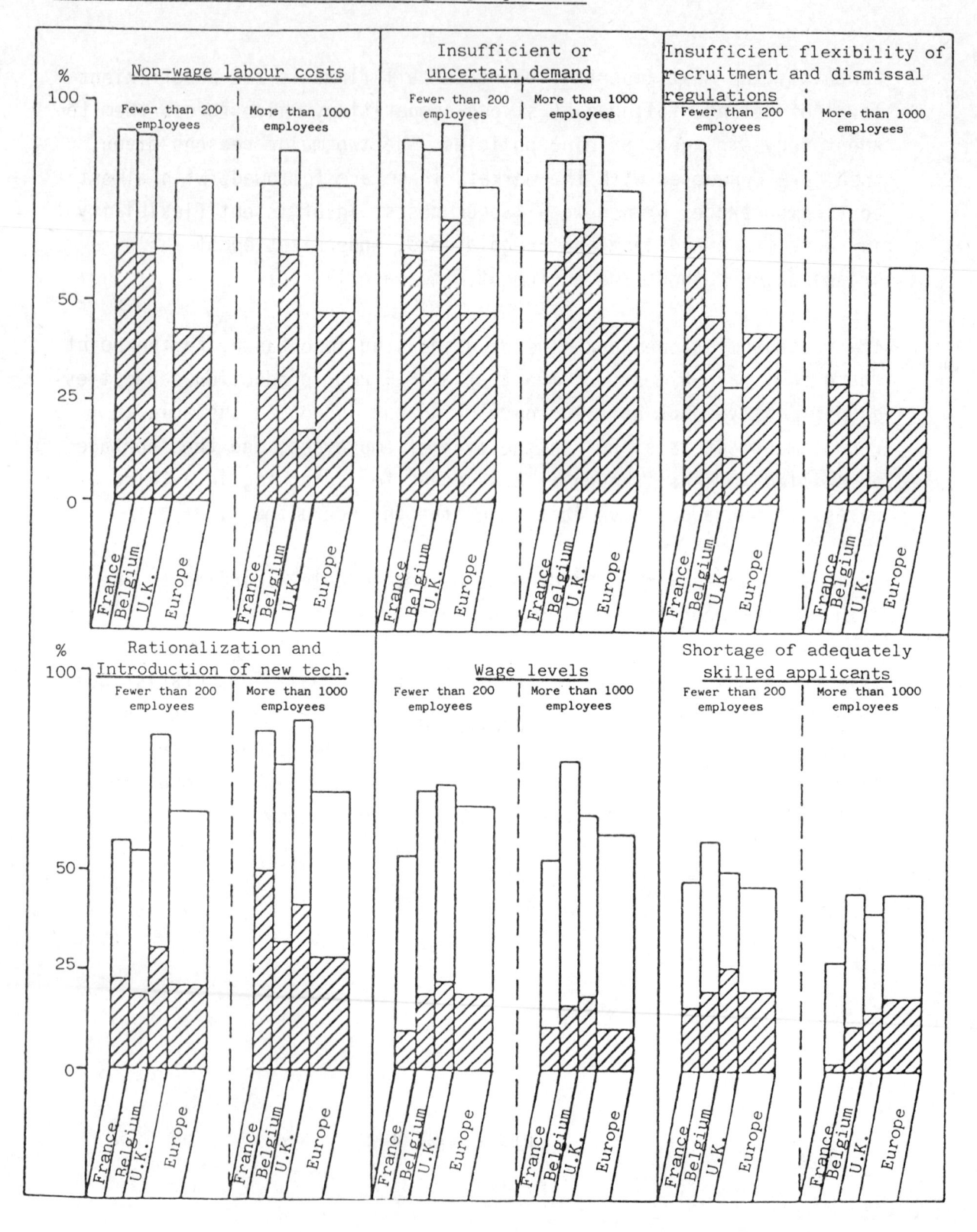

[Charts showing six reasons across France, Belgium, U.K., and Europe, for firms with fewer than 200 employees and more than 1000 employees:
- Non-wage labour costs
- Insufficient or uncertain demand
- Insufficient flexibility of recruitment and dismissal regulations
- Rationalization and Introduction of new tech.
- Wage levels
- Shortage of adequately skilled applicants]

Proportion of firms who cited these reasons as important ▨ or fairly important ☐ motives for not increasing staffing levels

* Of French firms with fewer than 200 employees, 63% cite non-wage labour costs as very important reasons for not increasing employment and 30% cite them as fairly important reasons.

The results relating to Europe are those of the Nine-Member States that took part in the survey

The diagram shows the part played by the size factor. It would appear that, on average, the size factor is of minor importance, except perhaps in the case of rationalization and the introduction of new technology. On the other hand, the weighting of the answers varies very considerably from country to country: in Italy and the UK, employers complain of the lack of demand, which is not the case in Germany or the Netherlands. The insufficient flexibility of recruitment and dismissal regulations seems to weigh very heavily in Italy, France and Belgium but is seldom mentioned in the UK.

Rationalization and the introduction of new technology are not, contrary to a very widespread belief, a decisive obstacle to recruitment.

c)   Relaxation of constraints... without a consensus

Demand and competition are areas in which national governments and the European Community can take action. Such actions are based on economic or industrial policy and their effects will be felt only in the medium term.

The next question posed to employers proposed a series of measures connected very specifically with "flexibility". Having recorded employers' opinions on existing situations, the next step was to gauge their opinions of measures likely to transform their employment plans.

The following diagram illustrates the averages of the answers.

Changes in the labour market: overall results

The question asked was:

Looking at the list of possible changes below, which effect do you think each might have on your employment plans for the next 12 months?

1. Shorter periods of notice and simpler legal procedures for dismissals
2. More frequent use of temporary contracts (interim work, fixed-term contracts, etc)
3. Better trained job-seekers
4. Introduction of wider wage differentials according to skills and working conditions
5. Greater emphasis on productivity in determining wages and salaries
6. Introduction of "initial wage rates" (ie lower wages for new starters)
7. More flexible working time arrangements at company level
8. Reduction of redundancy payments that may need to be made
9. Employment subsidies for recruiting certain categories of the unemployed
10. Functional improvement of public employment offices
11. Reduction in standard weekly working hours without increasing total production costs
12. Introduction of profit-oriented components in contractual salaries

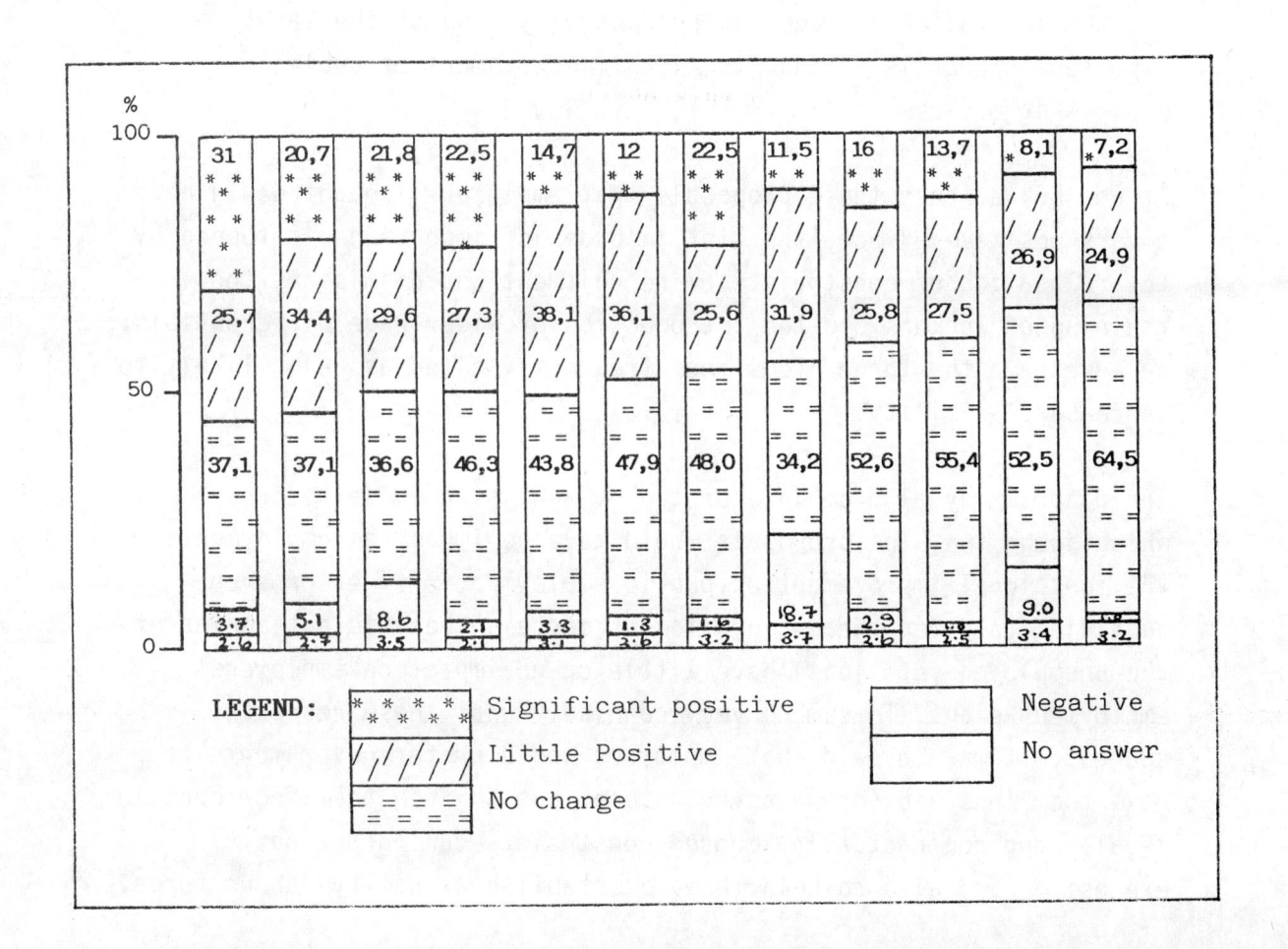

%												
100	31	20,7	21,8	22,5	14,7	12	22,5	11,5	16	13,7	8,1	7,2
	25,7	34,4	29,6	27,3	38,1	36,1	25,6	31,9	25,8	27,5	26,9	24,9
50	37,1	37,1	36,6	46,3	43,8	47,9	48,0	34,2	52,6	55,4	52,5	64,5
0	3.7 / 2.6	5.1 / 2.7	8.6 / 3.5	2.1 / 2.1	3.3 / 3.1	1.3 / 2.6	1.6 / 3.2	18.7 / 3.7	2.9 / 2.6	1.9 / 2.5	9.0 / 3.4	— / 3.2

LEGEND:
- * * * * Significant positive
- / / / / Little Positive
- = = = = No change
- ▭ Negative
- ▭ No answer

If we look, in order of decreasing importance, at the proposals likely to have a (very or little) positive effect on employment, we can see that greater flexibility for recruitment comes incontestably top of the list, followed by more frequent use of temporary contracts and the indexation of wages to productivity. One of the least important proposals is the functional improvement of public employment offices.

If we look at only those proposals that employers thought would have a very positive effect, the list in order of importance is topped by the relaxation of constraints on recruitment and dismissal, the training of workers and the introduction of wider wage differentials; here we have the three items most frequently cited as being likely to increase flexibility.

The diagram may also be interpreted by analysing those responses which judge that the proposals would have no impact on employment: the functional improvement of public employment offices or even subsidies (aid for the integration of certain specific categories of the unemployed into jobs) have little or no impact on employers' employment plans. To sum up very concisely what these responses suggest, it may be said that employers would prefer governments to give them less aid (of whatever nature) but to free them from certain legally and contractually imposed constraints during periods of expansion, and also to help them to establish a quality labour force.

It is also interesting to note the three measures which provoke very negative reactions: firstly, the reduction in working hours without increasing production costs. Here we have undoubtedly touched on one of the highly sensitive points as regards flexibility. The divergence from trade union opinion here is very marked. We should however treat these averages with some caution because there was a very wide variation in the answers to this question. Italian firms are extremely hostile to such a measure (62%), whereas it draws a negative response from only 7% of firms in the UK and France, 4% in the Netherlands and 3% in Ireland (Luxembourg, Belgium and Germany are in favour of the measure - 36% and 24% respectively).

The second measure that arouses very negative reactions is the introduction of an element linking pay and profit more closely; here too, Italy stands out on its own with a much higher percentage of hostile responses than any other European country.

Finally, the indexation of wages to productivity draws a negative reaction from 28% of British firms and 13% of Irish firms.

The responses to all these questions vary very considerably from country to country. The relaxation of constraints on recruitment seems to be an extremely desirable measure for 79% of Italian firms and 50% of Greek firms, while it would change nothing for 66% of firms in the UK.

French and Irish firms feel that the improvement of job-seekers' skills would have no impact on their recruitment decisions (75% and 85% respectively), whereas this factor would appear to be decisive for firms in Italy and Luxembourg (56%).

The graph on the following page clearly reveals the divergence of opinions held on this subject by firms in the various European countries. With a few slight differences, employers in the Netherlands, the UK and France feel that none of the proposed measures are likely to make them alter their employment plans. They feel that the crucial factors lie elsewhere, particularly in trends in demand. This opinion is not shared by Italian, Greek or, to a lesser extent, Belgian employers, who think on the contrary that such measures would radically alter their recruitment behaviour.

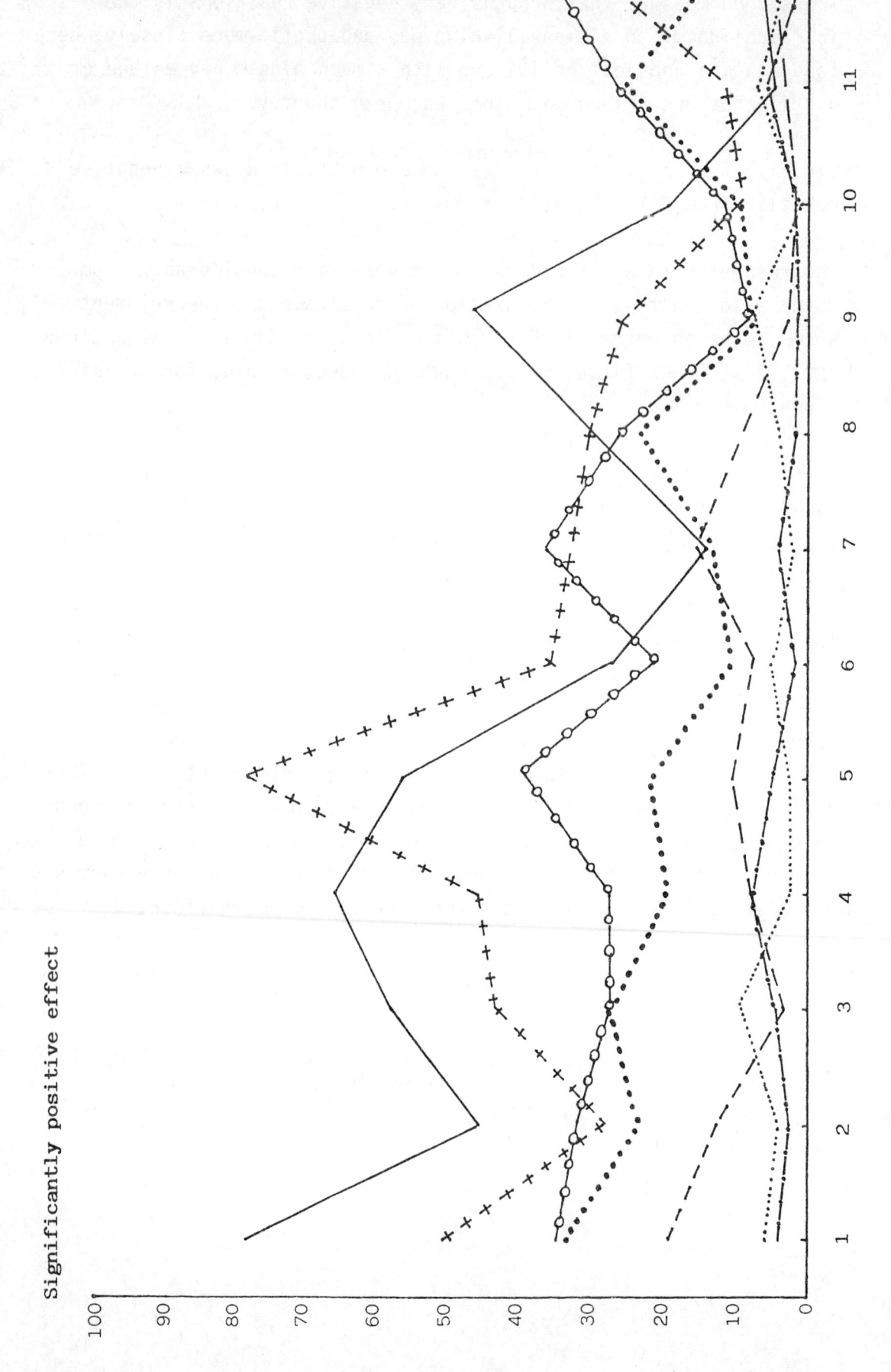

CHANGES IN THE LABOUR MARKET AND THEIR IMPACT ON EMPLOYMENT

Significantly positive effect

The numbers refer to the questions on page 73

The only conclusions we can draw from this set of responses are that:

- there is a fairly wide diversity of opinions, which can perhaps be partly explained both by the diversity of relevant regulations, as analysed by Professor Blampain, and doubtless also by differences in economic situations;

- there is no real unanimity on the effectiveness of any particular measure, even the measure which is the most widely approved and bears on the simplification of dismissal regulations, which was viewed favourably by 79% of Italian firms but by only 6% of British and Dutch firms and 4% of Irish firms;

- this analysis is confirmed by the responses to a complementary question which asked employers what the real effect of all the suggested measures would be on their employment plans over the next 12 months, with the answers giving both trends and percentages.

If we look at the trends, we can see that the differences already mentioned are accompanied by two anomalies, as revealed in the diagram on the following page.

Real effects of the changes described on your employment plans over the next 12 months

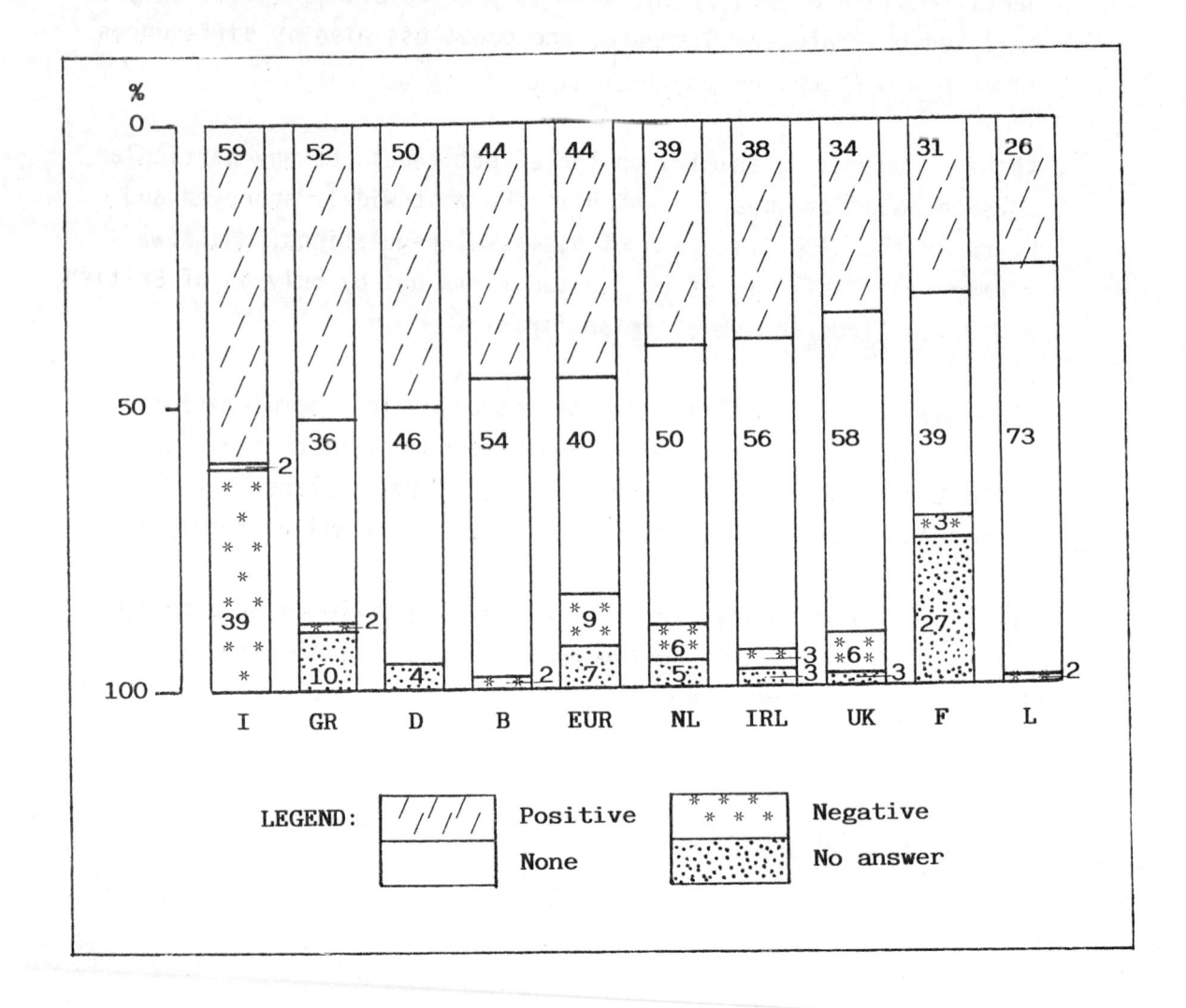

	I	GR	D	B	EUR	NL	IRL	UK	F	L
Positive	59	52	50	44	44	39	38	34	31	26
None	—	36	46	54	40	50	56	58	39	73
Negative	39	2	—	2	9	6	3	6	3	—
No answer	2	10	4	—	7	5	3	3	27	2

LEGEND: Positive / None / Negative / No answer

The proposed measures arouse both a very positive and a very negative response in Italy. This is the only country in which such wide discrepancies of opinion occur. The second special case is that of France, where the percentage of "no answers" is very high; this is no doubt a reflection of some uncertainty, or even strong doubts, as regards the measures likely to help increase employment.

Apart from predicting simple trends, employers were asked to estimate the figures involved in the upward or downward trends they anticipated (see graph below).

Net effect on employment, in percentages

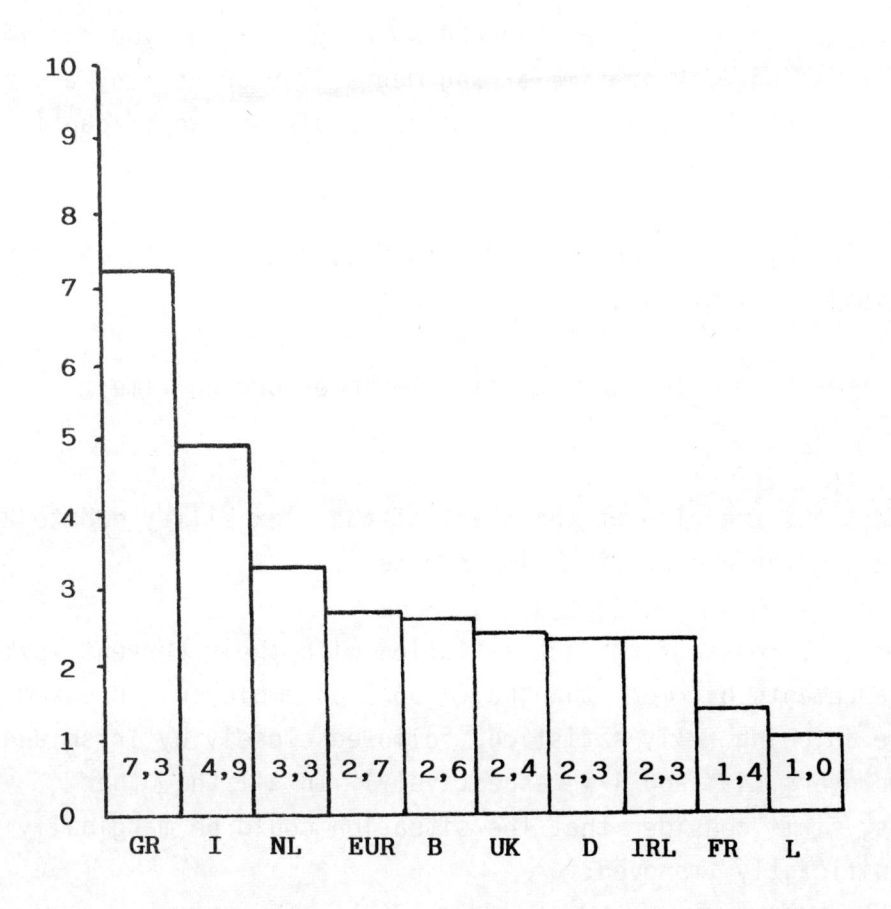

	GR	I	NL	EUR	B	UK	D	IRL	FR	L
	7,3	4,9	3,3	2,7	2,6	2,4	2,3	2,3	1,4	1,0

In all cases, the net effect is positive and reveals that, on average, firms would revise their employment plans upward by nearly 3%, though there are wide discrepancies between countries: more than 7% in Greece, as against just under 1 % in Luxembourg. This is obviously no more than an expression of opinions but should be taken into account in any consideration or action as regards employment.

d) Flexible working-time arrangements

Apart from the length of the standard working week, do you consider that the existing working-time arrangements in your company are fully satisfactory/could be marginally improved/could be significantly improved?

Has your company increased or is it about to increase significantly the flexibility of working time arrangements?

What are the reasons for and against flexible working time arrangements?

These questions are also at the heart of the flexibility debate and the answers given are of vital importance.

A quarter of European firms are satisfied with their current working time arrangements but more than half (58%) of employers in Luxembourg are alone in being fully satisfied, followed closely by Irish and Dutch employers (49% and 47% respectively). In all the other countries, firms consider that the situation could be marginally or even significantly improved.

Current working time arrangements

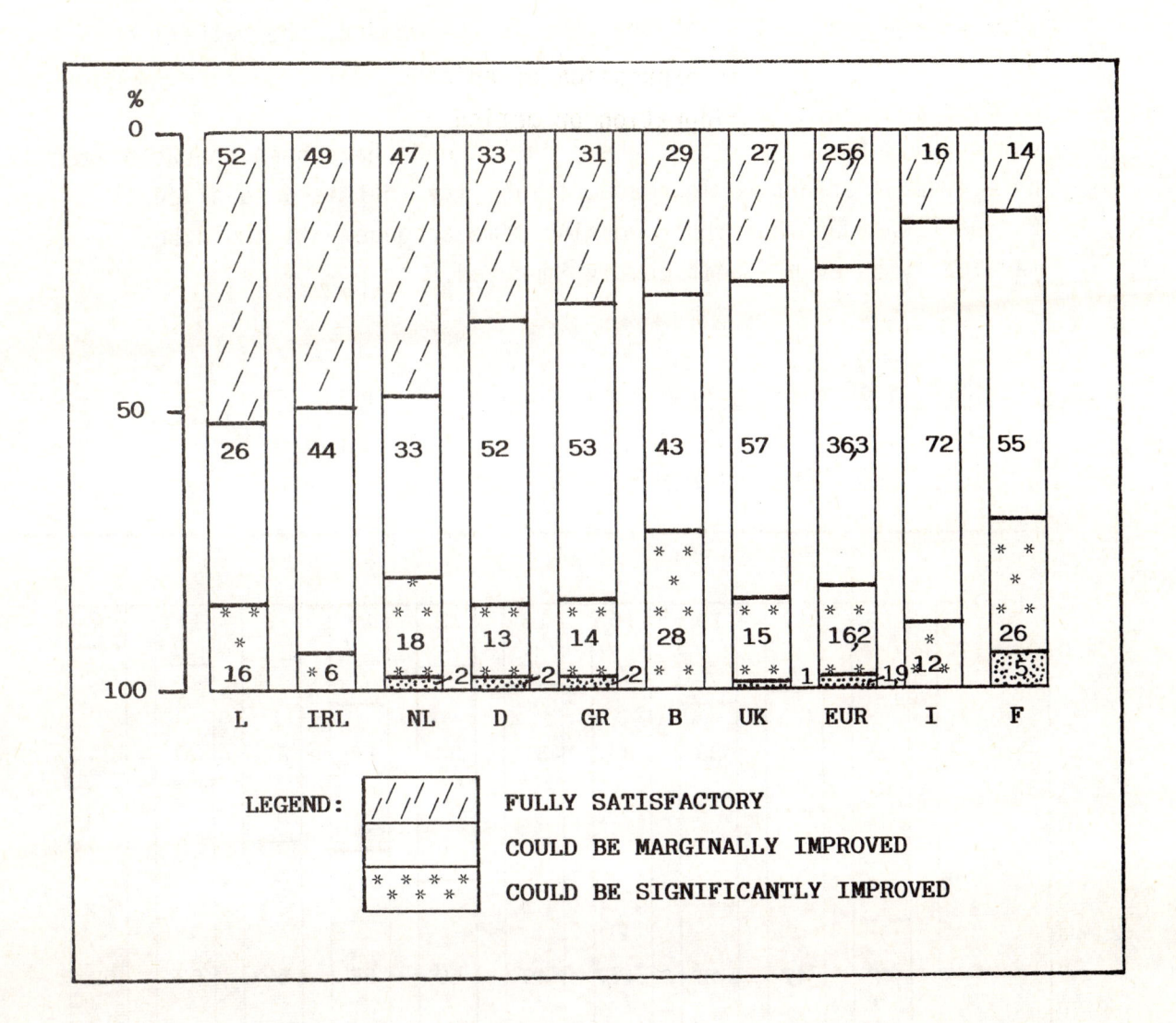

	L	IRL	NL	D	GR	B	UK	EUR	I	F
Fully satisfactory	52	49	47	33	31	29	27	25	16	14
Could be marginally improved	26	44	33	52	53	43	57	36	72	55
Could be significantly improved	16	6	18	13	14	28	15	16	12	26
			2	2	2		1	2		5

LEGEND:
- ///// FULLY SATISFACTORY
- (blank) COULD BE MARGINALLY IMPROVED
- ****   COULD BE SIGNIFICANTLY IMPROVED

Paradoxically, it was firms in countries where flexibility in working time arrangements had increased the least during the 2-3 years preceding the survey which were the most satisfied with their working time arrangements. This is the case in Luxembourg, the Netherlands and Ireland.

Conversely, firms in Italy, where past trends have been characterized by a general effort to increase flexibility that is unequalled in Europe, consider that their working time arrangements could be marginally or even significantly improved.

Flexibility of working time arrangements

Trend over the past 2-3 years

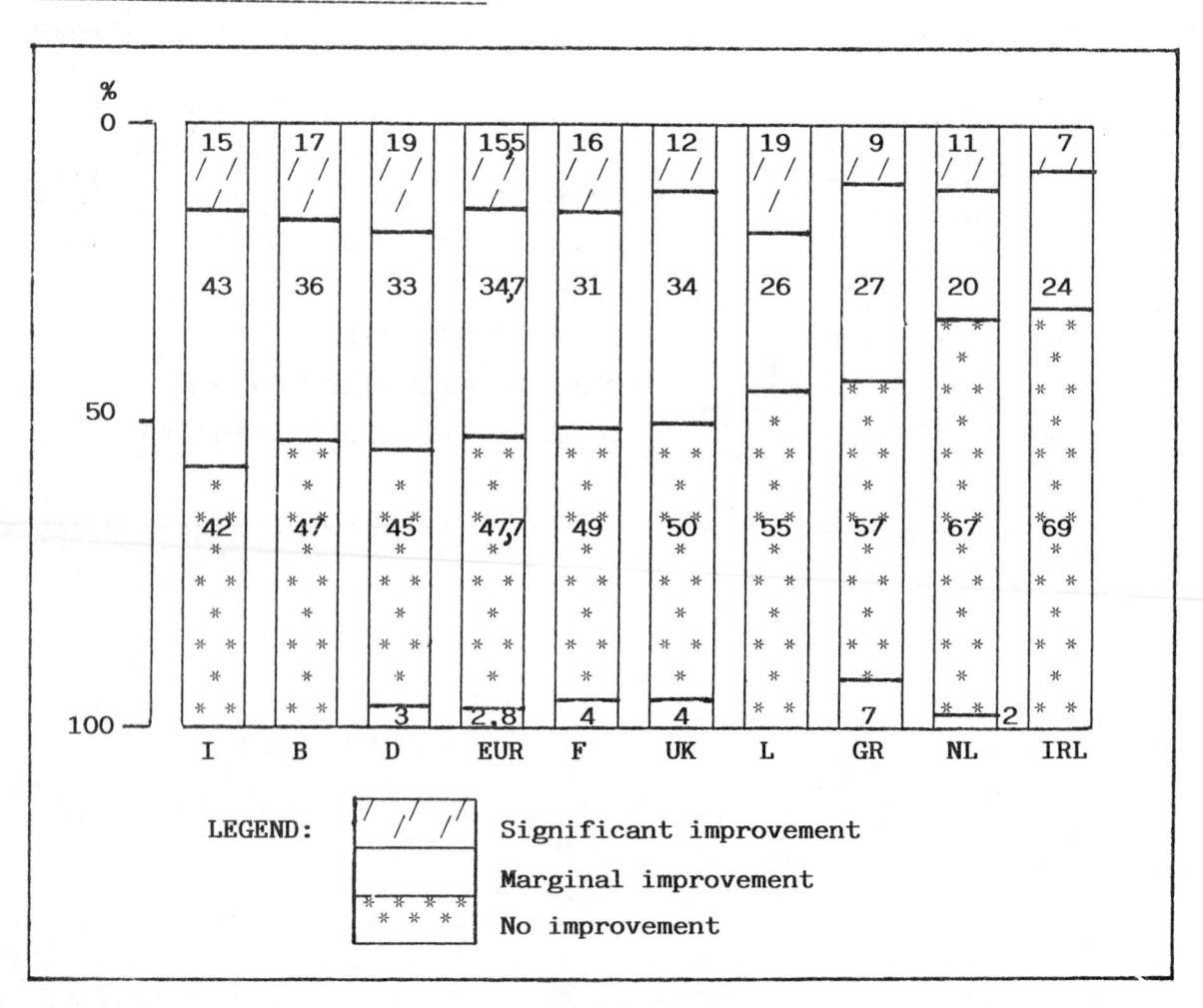

	I	B	D	EUR	F	UK	L	GR	NL	IRL
Significant improvement	15	17	19	15,5	16	12	19	9	11	7
Marginal improvement	43	36	33	34,7	31	34	26	27	20	24
No improvement	42	47	45	47,7	49	50	55	57	67	69
			3	2,8	4	4		7	2	

LEGEND:
- /// Significant improvement
- Marginal improvement
- *** No improvement

Employers' forecasts do nothing more than project the past into the future, as the diagram below illustrates.

Flexibility of working time arrangements

Trend over the next 2-3 years

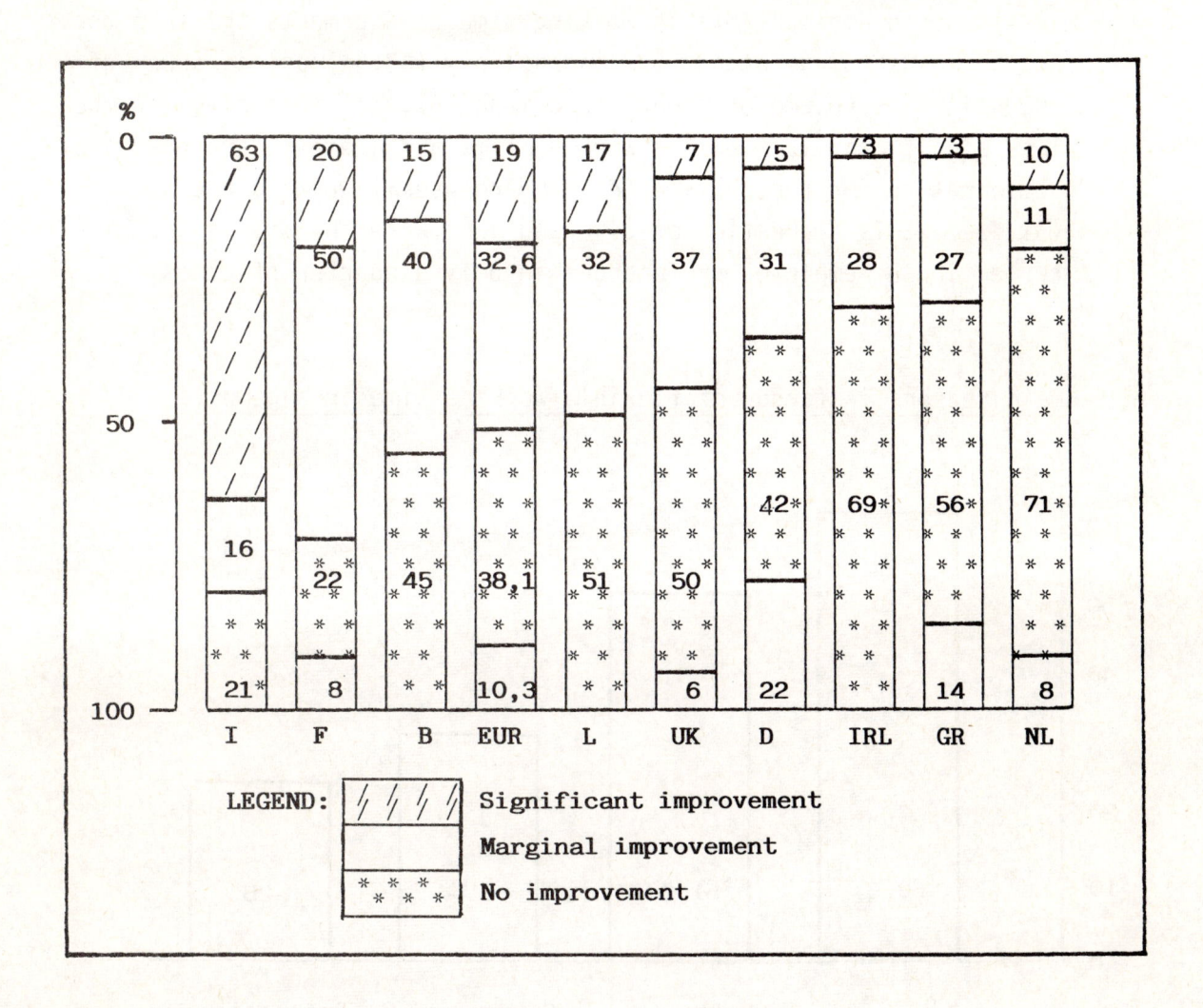

	I	F	B	EUR	L	UK	D	IRL	GR	NL
Significant improvement	63	20	15	19	17	7	5	3	3	10
Marginal improvement	16	50	40	32,6	32	37	31	28	27	11
No improvement (middle)		22	45	38,1	51	50	42	69	56	71
No improvement (bottom)	21	8		10,3		6	22		14	8

LEGEND:
- /// Significant improvement
- Marginal improvement
- *** No improvement

Dutch and Irish employers did not anticipate any increase in the flexibility of working time arrangements in the next 2-3 years, whereas by contrast, and furthermore in compliance with what actually happened, Italian and French firms envisaged much greater flexibility in working-time arrangements.

In order to understand these opinions, we can analyse the reasons put forward by firms to justify their support of, or opposition to, more flexible working time.

First and foremost, flexible working-time arrangements are seen both as the means to use plant more intensively (62.5%) and as a way of adjusting the volume of labour to demand (51.2%). Secondly, and much less significantly, flexible working-time arrangements are the usual compensation for a reduction in standard weekly working hours (31.4%). It is a question of give and take. Flexibility is the reflection of employee preferences in only a quarter of cases.

Main reasons in favour of flexible working-time arrangements

Better utilization of plant	Better adjustment to demand	Compensation for reduction in working hours	Reflection of employee preference
62,5	51,2	31,4	25

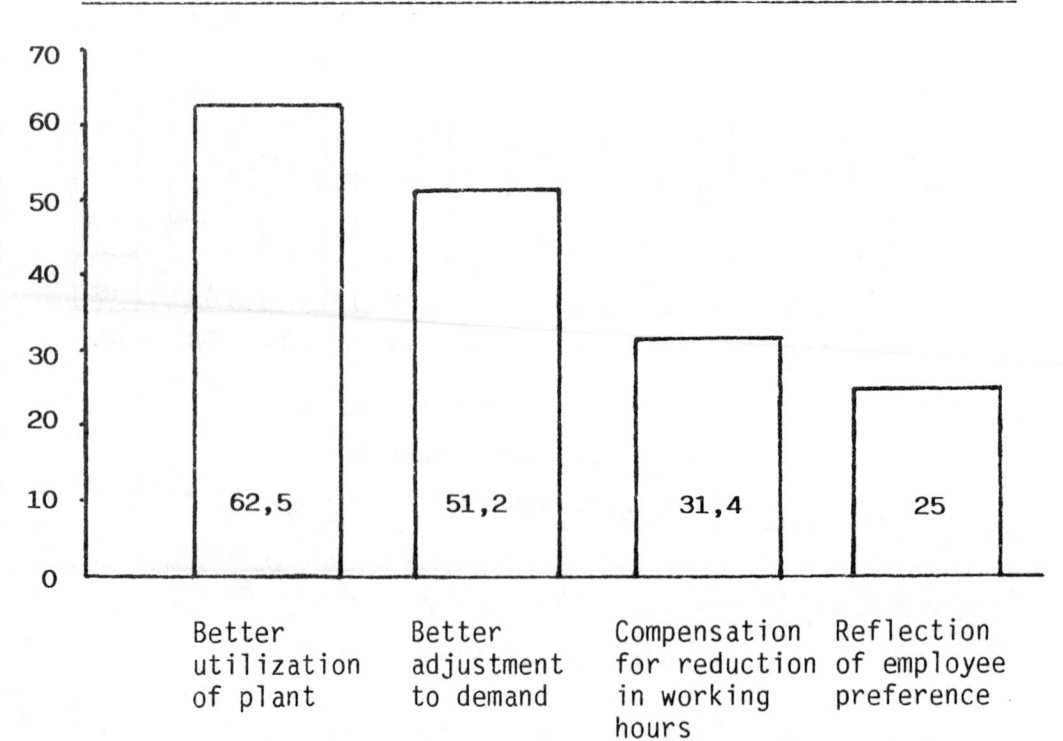

Main reasons against flexible working-time arrangements

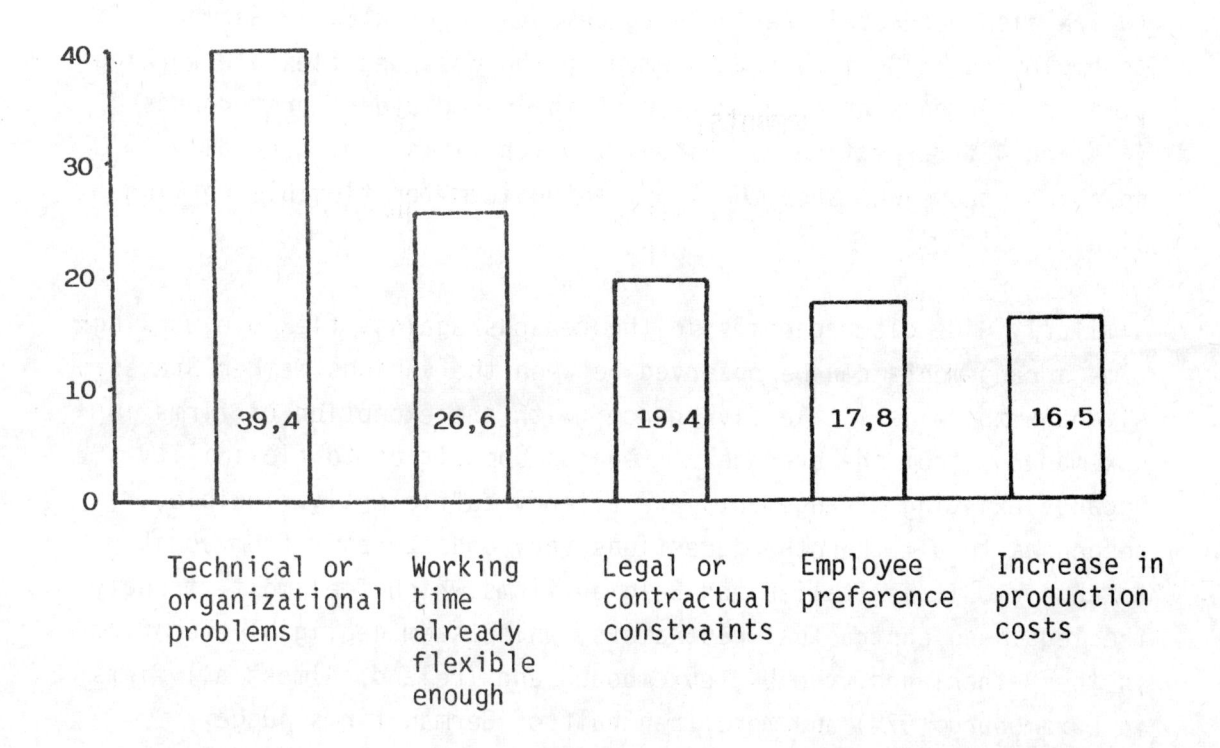

Reason	%
Technical or organizational problems	39,4
Working time already flexible enough	26,6
Legal or contractual constraints	19,4
Employee preference	17,8
Increase in production costs	16,5

The reasons against flexible working-time arrangements are primarily linked with technical and organizational constraints (39.4%). Working time cannot be made more flexible because it simply is not possible. This does not imply any disagreement with the general idea of flexible working time arrangements. Secondly, more than a quarter of firms consider that their working-time arrangements are already sufficiently flexible to meet their needs. Thirdly, some firms claim that they cannot make working time more flexible because of legal or contractual restrictions which prevent them from doing so (19.4%) or because their employees are against it (17.8%). Finally, 16.5% of firms consider that flexible working-time arrangements would increase their production costs.

Once again, these averages hide huge discrepancies between countries (see table in the Annex). Italian employers are in favour of flexible working times for two essential reasons: more intensive use of plant (91%) and better adjustment to demand (86%). Employees' preferences

only account for 4%. As many as 66% of German firms see flexible
working times as a compensation for a reduction in working hours
(which also accurately reflects agreements negotiated in Germany).It
is employers in Germany and Luxembourg who most see flexible working-
time arrangements as a reflection of their employees' preferences
(46% and 42% respectively). Finally, Dutch firms are, generally
speaking, those who show the least enthusiasm for flexible working
times.

Similarly wide discrepancies in the reasons against flexible working-
time arrangements can be observed between the various Member States.
Although there is little divergence (with the exception of firms in
Luxembourg) from the average as regards opposition to flexibility
because existing arrangements are already sufficiently flexible,
responses to all the other questions vary considerably from country
to country. It is Italian and Belgian firms which feel most strongly
the legal and contractual restraints, which seem negligible for firms
in the Netherlands, the UK, Luxembourg and Ireland. Almost all firms
in Luxembourg (97%) and more than half of German firms judge
technical and/or organizational problems to be the root of their
inability to introduce flexible working-time arrangements. A third of
Belgian employers consider such arrangements to be impossible because
of employee preferences, whereas this reason is very insignificant
for their counterparts in the Netherlands and Luxembourg.

e)   ... and job-sharing

Do you think any of the full-time jobs in your firm could be split
into part-time jobs without significant economic disadvantages for
your firm?

Though the majority response to this question was in the negative,
the graph on the following page shows that there were only a few more
"no" than "yes" answers.

Job-sharing

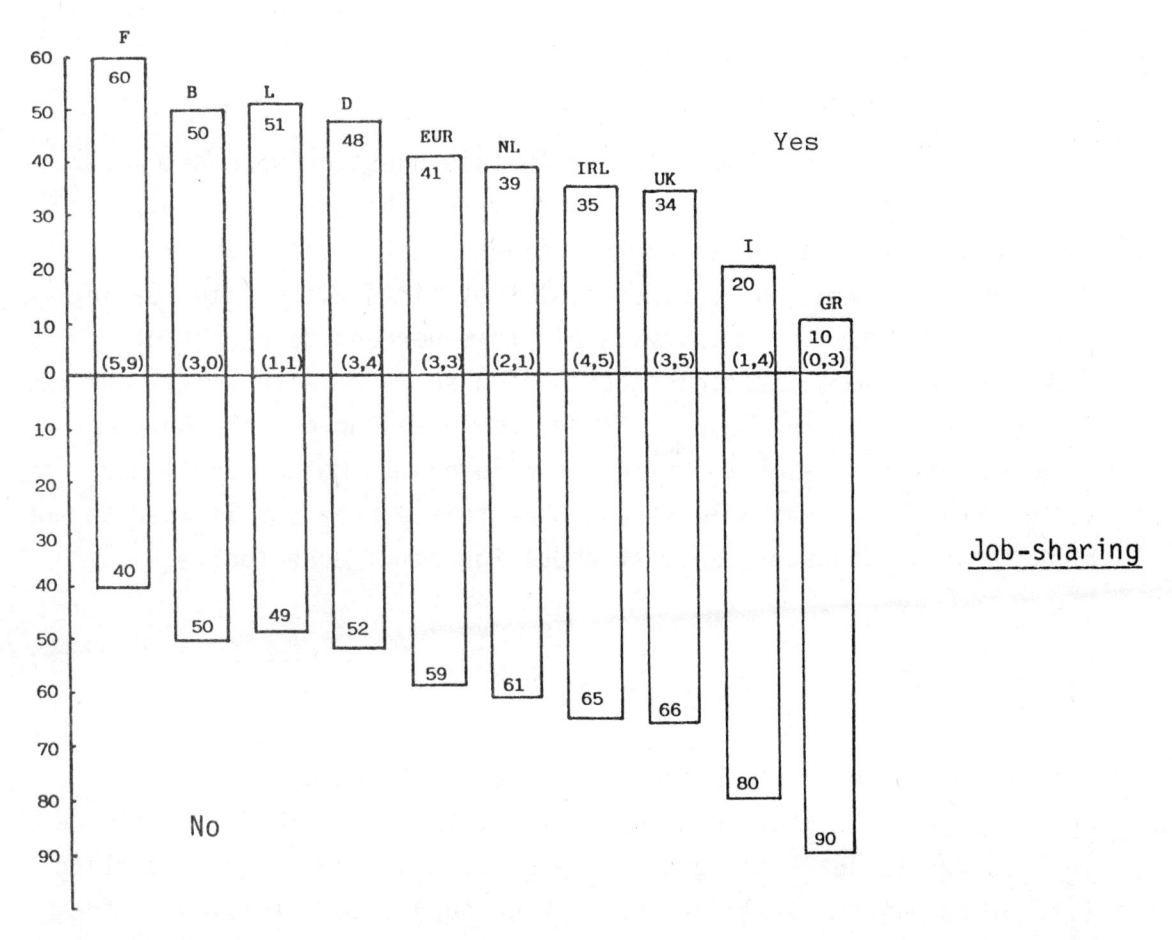

Country	Yes	No	(avg % of jobs that could be split)
F	60	40	(5,9)
B	50	50	(3,0)
L	51	49	(1,1)
D	48	52	(3,4)
EUR	41	59	(3,3)
NL	39	61	(2,1)
IRL	35	65	(4,5)
UK	34	66	(3,5)
I	20	80	(1,4)
GR	10	90	(0,3)

The bracketed figures are the average percentages of jobs that could be split.

As in the case of all the other questions, answers varied widely from country to country. Thus French firms were the most in favour of splitting jobs, though this may well be due to the fact that half-time working, which has taken a long time to develop in France, is now increasing in leaps and bounds; the same explanation could apply to Belgium (see the table in Part 1 which indicates the extent and composition of part-time working). The paradox is in fact that it is those countries with the lowest percentage of part-time jobs, ie Greece and Italy (5.3% as against 24% in the Netherlands), which are the most hostile to the idea of splitting jobs (it should be remembered that these are also the countries where opinion was most in favour of flexible working time). This reaction also indicates the extent to which opinions are cyclical and determined, at least in part, by the economic environment.

Firms who gave a positive response to this question were asked to state the number of full-time jobs they thought could be "split in two". The average alone is worth considering as more than 3% of existing full-time jobs could be split by firms without increasing their overheads. At Community level, this percentage represents 800 000 full-time jobs. This supply is also faced with a real demand, as is revealed by the results of the employee survey; the only question which remains to be answered is how to match supply and demand. Finally, we should stress that this survey was limited to the manufacturing industry. So what about the service sector?

2. Wholesale and retail trade

The survey of the distribution sector was conducted in just five Member States: Belgium, France, Germany, the Netherlands and the UK. This survey is interesting not only because of the large proportion (15% at Community level) of the working population employed in the sector, but also because it covers branches whose constraints are theoretically very different from those suffered by the manufacturing industry and, above all, because it is a sector reputed to be creating jobs, even in the current economic situation. Firms in this sector were asked exactly the same questions as industrial firms, with a few specific questions added.

a) Background: wait and see

Despite the expected growth in consumption, firms in this sector do not plan to increase recruitment, with the exception of a few firms which even then would expect only a slight increase. German firms in both the wholesale and the retail trade are by far the most pessimistic, followed by Belgian and French firms; Dutch and British firms are considerably more optimistic.

Overall, large firms (with more than 50 employees) are both more optimistic and more pessimistic than small firms (see table in the Annex).

b) <u>Lower wages for new starters rather than reduced working hours</u>

Wholesale and retail firms have almost identical reactions to the various measures which, if implemented, might change their recruitment behaviour.

Two measures arouse a very or fairly positive response from both retail and wholesale firms: the relaxation of government constraints on dismissal and lower initial wage rates. These are followed by the measure concerning the introduction of wage differentials according to skills and working conditions. The opinions of retail and wholesale firms then diverge on the usefulness of more flexible working time as a means of creating jobs: nearly 40% of retail firms believe that flexible working-time arrangements could be a positive factor in job creation, while barely more than 30% of wholesale firms hold the same belief.

Legend to the two diagrams and two graphs on the following pages:

Question:

Looking at the list of possible changes below, what effect do you think each might have on your employment plans for the next 12 months?

1. Introduction of special wage rates for job-starters
2. Relaxation of regulations on dismissals
3. Wage differentials according to skills and working conditions
4. Flexible working-time arrangements at company level
5. Employment subsidies
6. Temporary contracts
7. Linking of wages with profits
8. More flexible opening hours
9. Better trained job-seekers
10. Reduction in redundancy payments
11. Reduction in standard weekly working hours (cost-neutral)
12. Improvement of public employment offices

Changes in the labour market and their impact on employment

Retail trade

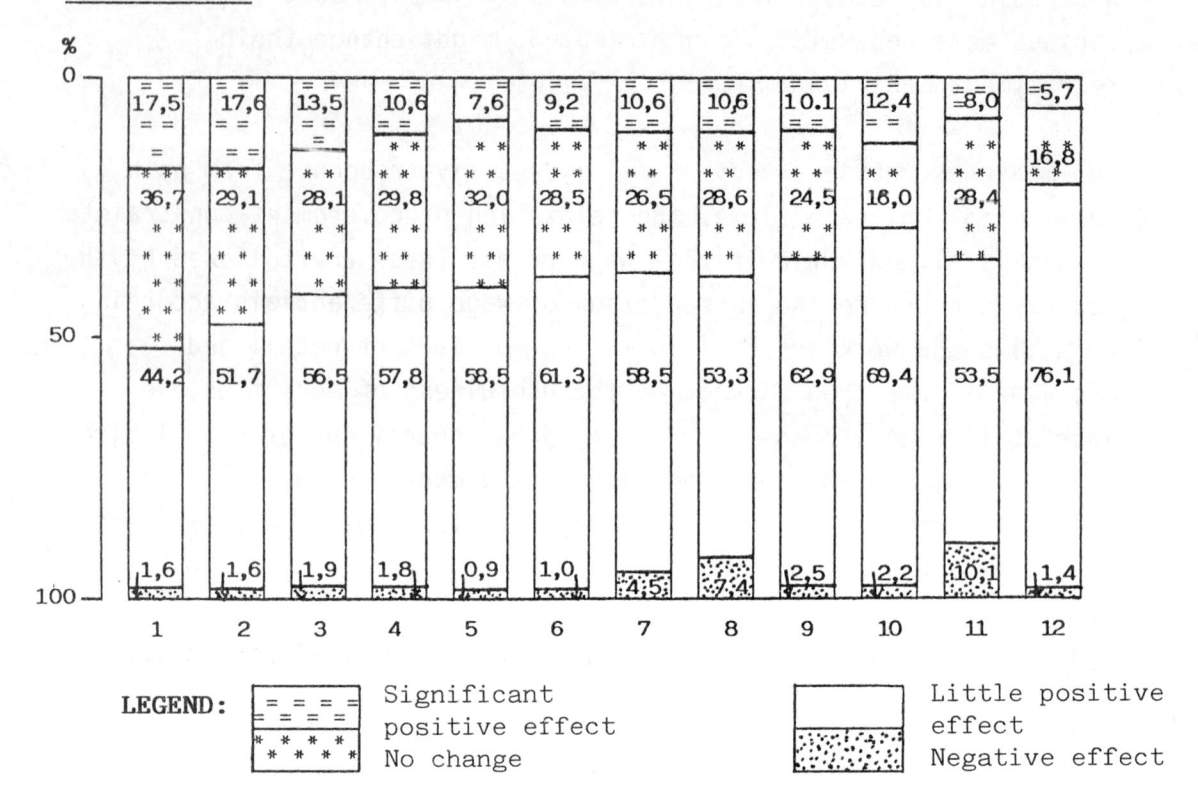

	1	2	3	4	5	6	7	8	9	10	11	12
Significant positive effect	17,5	17,6	13,5	10,6	7,6	9,2	10,6	10,6	10,1	12,4	8,0	5,7
No change	36,7	29,1	28,1	29,8	32,0	28,5	26,5	28,6	24,5	18,0	28,4	16,8
Little positive effect	44,2	51,7	56,5	57,8	58,5	61,3	58,5	53,3	62,9	69,4	53,5	76,1
Negative effect	1,6	1,6	1,9	1,8	0,9	1,0	4,5	7,4	2,5	2,2	10,1	1,4

LEGEND:
- ==== Significant positive effect
- **** No change
- ▯ Little positive effect
- ▒ Negative effect

Wholesale trade

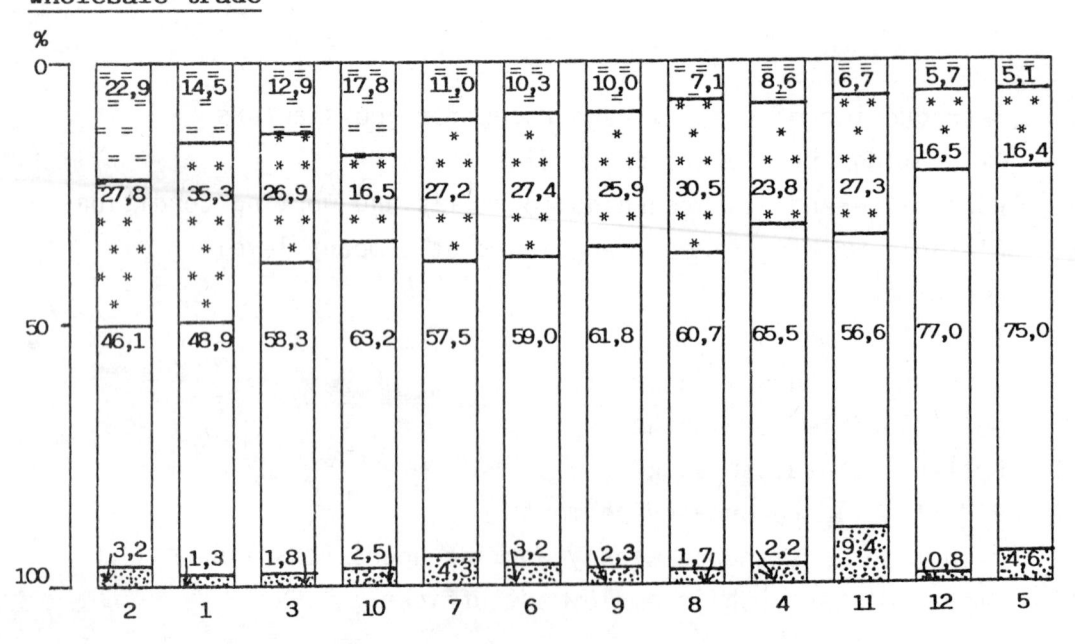

	2	1	3	10	7	6	9	8	4	11	12	5
Significant positive effect	22,9	14,5	12,9	17,8	11,0	10,3	10,0	7,1	8,6	6,7	5,7	5,1
No change	27,8	35,3	26,9	16,5	27,2	27,4	25,9	30,5	23,8	27,3	16,5	16,4
Little positive effect	46,1	48,9	58,3	63,2	57,5	59,0	61,8	60,7	65,5	56,6	77,0	75,0
Negative effect	3,2	1,3	1,8	2,5	4,3	3,2	2,3	1,7	2,2	9,4	0,8	4,6

Retail trade - significant positive effect

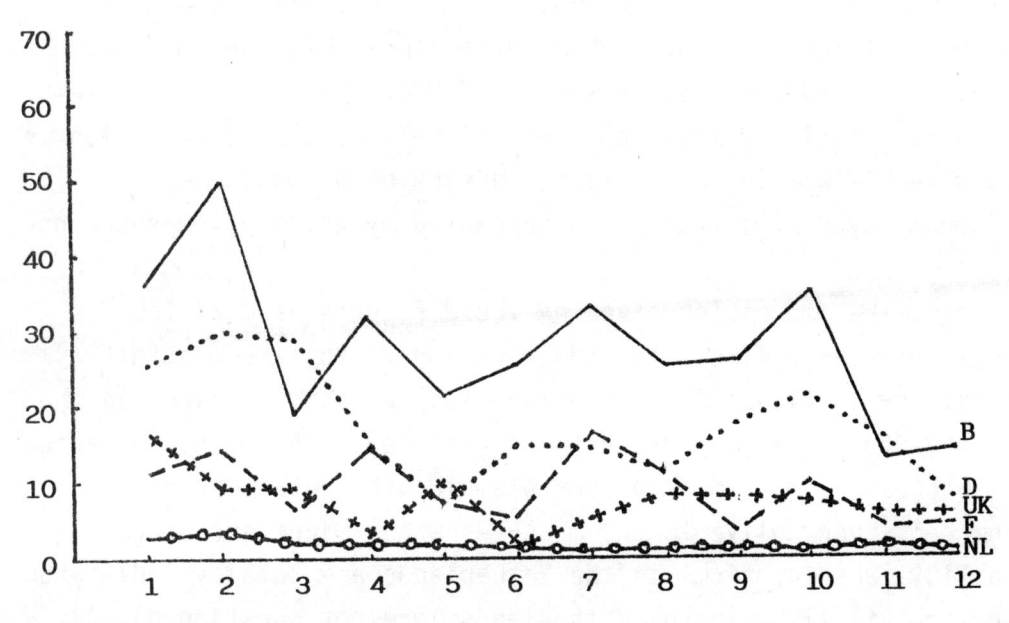

Wholesale trade - significant positive effect

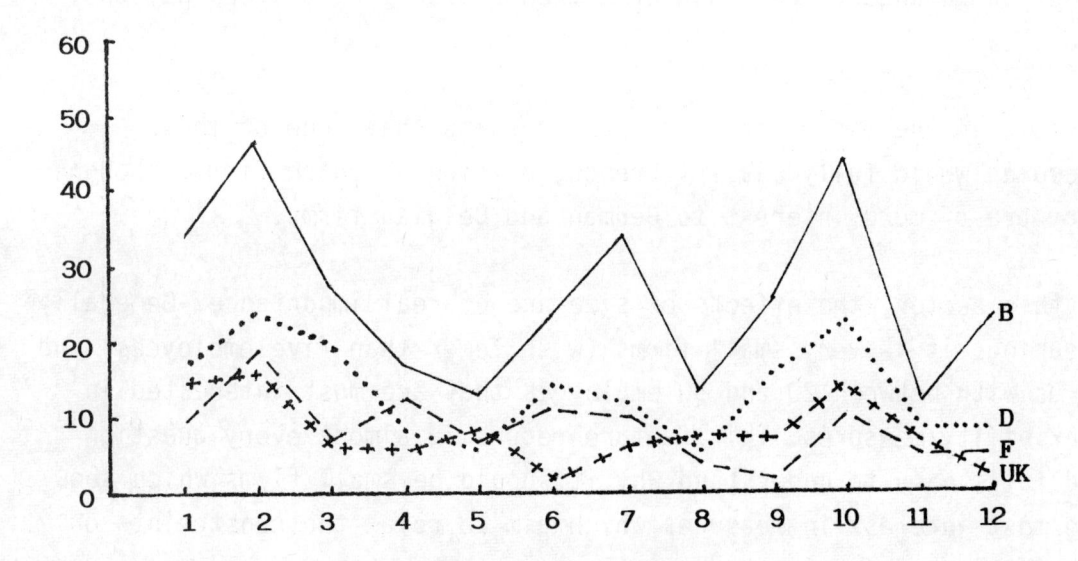

Overall, and as the graphs on the preceding pages illustrate, not one of the measures suggested attracts real approval. Just 17% of retail firms believe that the introduction of initial wage rates or the lifting of constraints on dismissal are likely to have a very positive effect on employment. Wholesale firms are a little more positive about the relaxation of government restrictions or the lowering of redundancy pay (22.9% and 17.8%). Finally, 10% of firms in both the retail and wholesale sectors believe that a reduction in standard weekly working hours might in fact be an obstacle to recruitment, even if it was not accompanied by any pay compensation.

On average, the impression given by these figures is that few measures are really likely to induce employers to take on staff. There is very little difference of opinion between employers in the retail and wholesale sectors, but the differences between the various Member States are more marked. For example, the retail trade in Belgium seems very alive to any measures which might encourage flexibility, whereas firms in the Netherlands are totally indifferent to them (retail firms in the Netherlands were not questioned). Belgian firms are very much in favour of the removal of obstacles to dismissal, whether it is a question of making procedures easier or reducing redundancy pay, and of a much closer link between pay and profits.

It is nevertheless clear from these results that none of these measures would fully satisfy French, British or Dutch firms, though they are of more interest to German and Belgian firms.

In this sector, the effects of size are of real importance. Generally speaking, it is very small firms (with fewer than five employees) and firms with between 20 and 50 employees that are most interested in flexibility measures. This feature recurs in almost every question and it is easy to understand why it should be small firms which show the most interest in measures which aim to relax the constraints on dismissal, reduce redundancy pay, etc.

Given these opinions, it is not surprising that it is Belgian wholesale and retail firms which think that, if these measures were actually implemented, they would lead to a 5% upward revision of employment plans. But then there is a big difference between making plans and putting them into effect.

c) <u>Ultimately satisfactory opening hours... which could be completely deregulated</u>

Overall, firms are happy with their opening hours. Paradoxically, they are happier with opening hours if they belong to the retail rather than the wholesale trade and are even more satisfied with them if they are small firms.

The most satisfied, those who would change nothing, are Dutch firms (though this might be expected following the results of the preceding question), whereas Belgian and British firms would prefer greater flexibility in their opening hours - preferably complete deregulation, but they would nonetheless accept a maximum limit within which firms would be free to structure their own opening hours.

d) <u>And, as in manufacturing industry, why not job-sharing?</u>

Finally, it is on the question of splitting jobs that retail and wholesale firms have the most favourable opinion. Here too, when considering the average, we have to bear in mind the fluctuations of opinion depending on the nationality and size of firms.

Nearly 55% of retail firms and 65% of wholesale firms are in favour of splitting their permanent jobs (it should be pointed out that the retail trade has the highest percentage of part-time workers).

In the retail trade, it is Dutch (75%) and British (64%) firms which are the most positive on this subject, with German and British firms being the most positive in the wholesale sector. Belgian firms, which are the most in favour of flexibility as a means of creating jobs, are much less in favour of splitting jobs. In both sectors, it is very small firms which claim to be the most in favour of this measure.

The percentage of full-time jobs which could be split varies both from country to country and depending on the size of the firm, but the averages are 6% in the retail sector and 2.7% in the wholesale sector, which overall represents a far from negligible number of jobs.

e) <u>What conclusions can we draw from this rather hazy picture?</u>

Perhaps we should first make a detour via France, where this survey of firms has been used for an analysis (Elbaum, 1987).

On the basis of the questions bearing on the impact of measures likely to increase the flexibility of the labour market, a typology of firms was drawn up by means of a computerized classification system. This classification reveals five different types of attitude to these flexibility measures (see table on the following page).

Typology	% per category	Size of firms	Sector	Financial situation	Preferred measures
Silent	26% of industrial firms	Industry: small firms - 60% have fewer than 200 employees. Commerce: 55% of firms with fewer than 5 employees and 80% of firms with fewer than 20 employees.	Consumer goods		
Indifferent	21% of retail shops	Industry: very large firms (+1000). Commerce: very small firms.	Cars Intermediate goods	Number of jobs decreasing Number of jobs stable	
Uncertain	37% of industry 45% of commerce	Industry: firms with 500-1000 employees. Large-scale businesses.			
Interested	37% of industry	Medium-sized firms.			
Very interested	34% of commerce	Industry: small firms with fewer than 200 employees.	Capital goods		Simplification of dismissal and flexible working-time arrangements.

This typology particularly highlights the fact that, at the time of the survey, only just over one-third of firms were interested or very interested in the suggested measures. The same percentage of industrial firms and 45% of retail firms were uncertain, and a quarter of firms either did not express any opinion and remained silent in the turmoil or were indifferent to the call of flexibility.

The size and sector of activity of firms go a long way toward explaining attitudes, as we can see if we look more closely at each group.

Typology of firms* (breakdown by size)
A. Industry

	Silent	Indifferent	Uncertain	Interested	Very interested
<200 employees	59	20	26	37	49
200–1000 employees	24	17	28	31	21
>1000 employees	17	63	46	32	30

11% of workforce — 15% — 37% — 26% — 11%

Firms with fewer than 200 employees
Firms with 200-1000 employees
Firms with more than 1000 employees

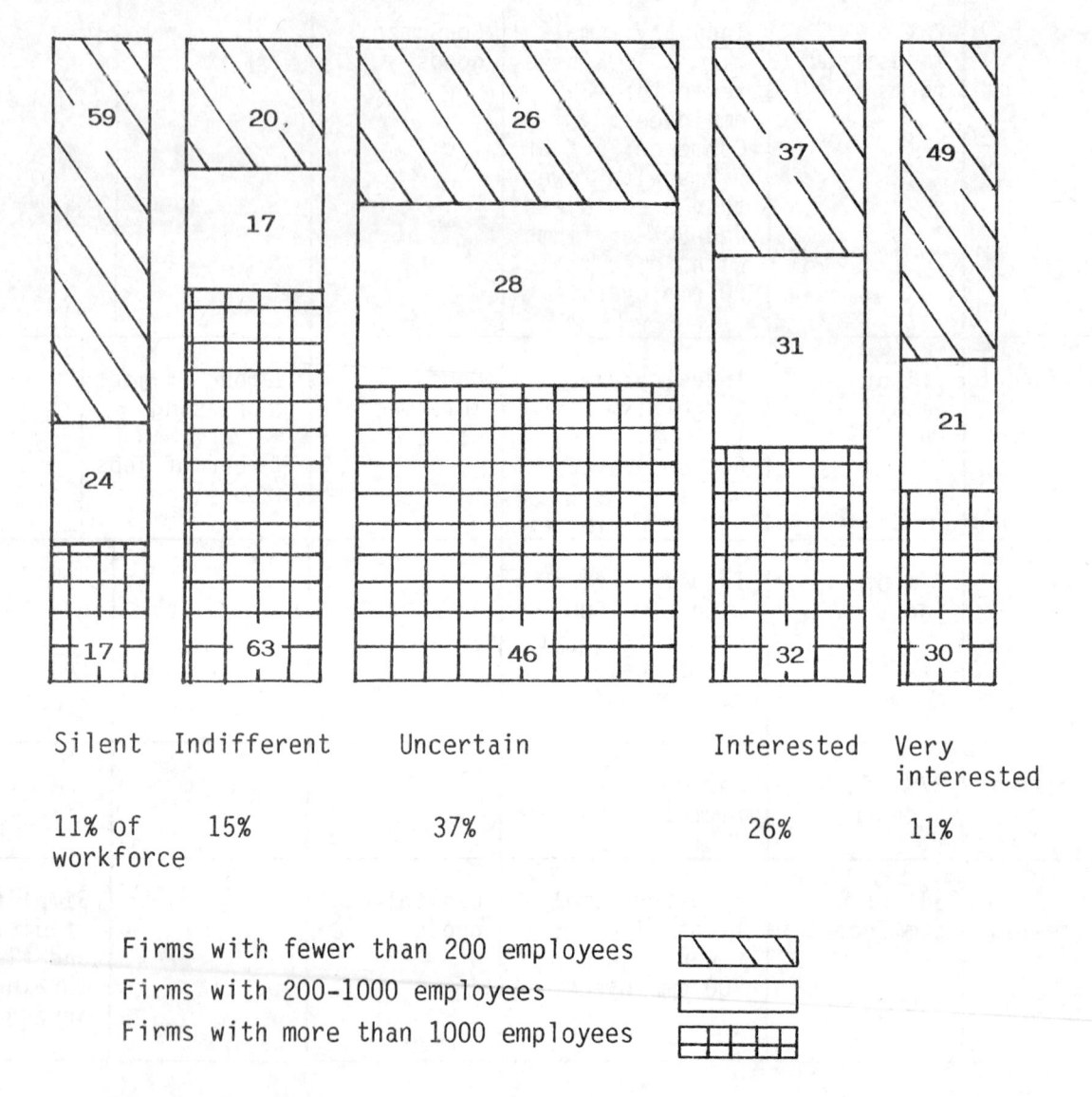

1. Employment trend over two years, obtained by comparing staffing levels for 1984 and 1985 with forecasts for 1986. Where staffing levels vary by less than 2.5% in absolute value in 1985 (1.4% in commerce), employment is said to be "stable". The graph indicates only those trends which differ substantially from the average for all firms in the same size group. For example, there is a drop in staffing levels of more than 2.5% over two years for 77% of firms with more than 1000 employees, but 85% of them are "incredulous".

* The method by which the typology was constructed is described in the notes to Table 2.

B. Retail trade

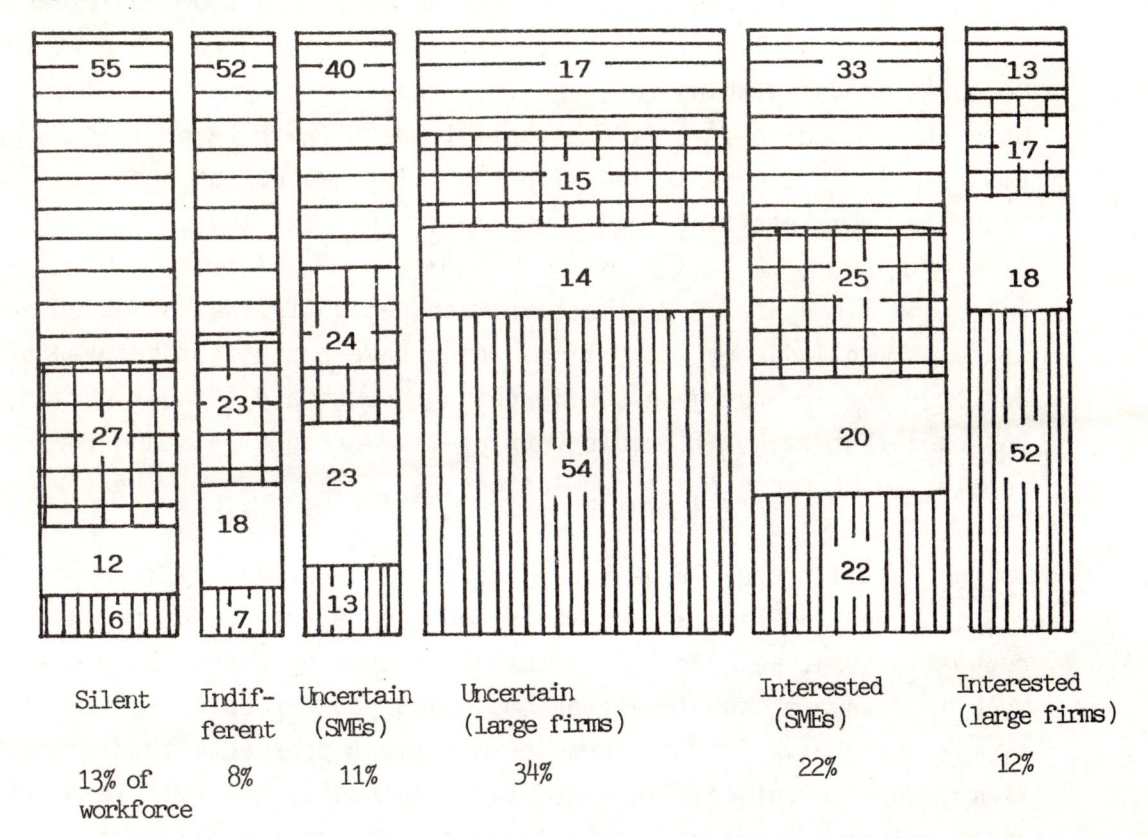

	Silent	Indifferent	Uncertain (SMEs)	Uncertain (large firms)	Interested (SMEs)	Interested (large firms)
Top	55	52	40	17	33	13
				15		17
	27	23	24	14	25	18
		18	23	54	20	52
	12				22	
	6	7	13			
% workforce	13%	8%	11%	34%	22%	12%

Legend:
- Firms with fewer than 5 employees
- Firms with 5-20 employees
- Firms with 20-200 employees
- Firms with more than 200 employees

The silent ones in both industry and commerce are small firms; in industry, there is a strong likelihood for these firms to belong to the consumer-goods sector.

Indifferent firms expect no positive effect on employment if the suggested measures were implemented, but their reasons are very different in industry and in commerce.

In industry, it is the large firms (with more than 1000 employees) that are in a difficult financial situation which do not expect these measures to do anything to check the drop in employment levels, whereas in commerce, it is the small traders (with fewer than 20 employees) who are satisfied with their lot and do not want to increase their staffing levels who adopt this attitude.

Uncertain firms are very selective with regard to the suggested measures: in industry, many firms which have a staff of between 500 and 1000 and are not necessarily going through a difficult period are the ones that favour flexible working-time arrangements and the relaxation of recruitment regulations.

In the retail trade, large-scale businesses are equally keen on flexible working-time arrangements and the relaxation of recruitment regulations, as well as the extension of opening hours. They are very much in favour of subsidies for employing young people. Medium-sized firms, which have less favourable employment prospects than large firms, show an interest in fixed-term contracts, the relaxation of dismissal procedures and the introduction of an initial wage rate.

Interested firms. In industry, a top group of firms is optimistic about the possible effect of the proposed measures, with some reservations about a few of them. They are in favour of flexibility "in volume": the relaxation of recruitment and dismissal procedures and flexible working-time arrangements.

Very interested firms tend to be small firms (with fewer than 200 employees) in the capital goods sector. Their only reservations with regard to the proposed measures concern the improvement of public employment offices or subsidies for the recruitment of the long-term unemployed, as well as the reduction of working hours.

Traders are never "very interested", but small and medium-sized firms are less selective than large distribution firms about the proposed measures and more certain that they would be likely to encourage recruitment (see charts on following pages).

Typology of firms: attitude to measures likely to increase employment flexibility

Question:
What effect would the following changes have on your current employment forecasts?

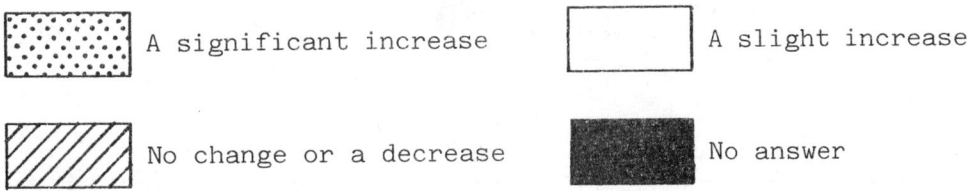

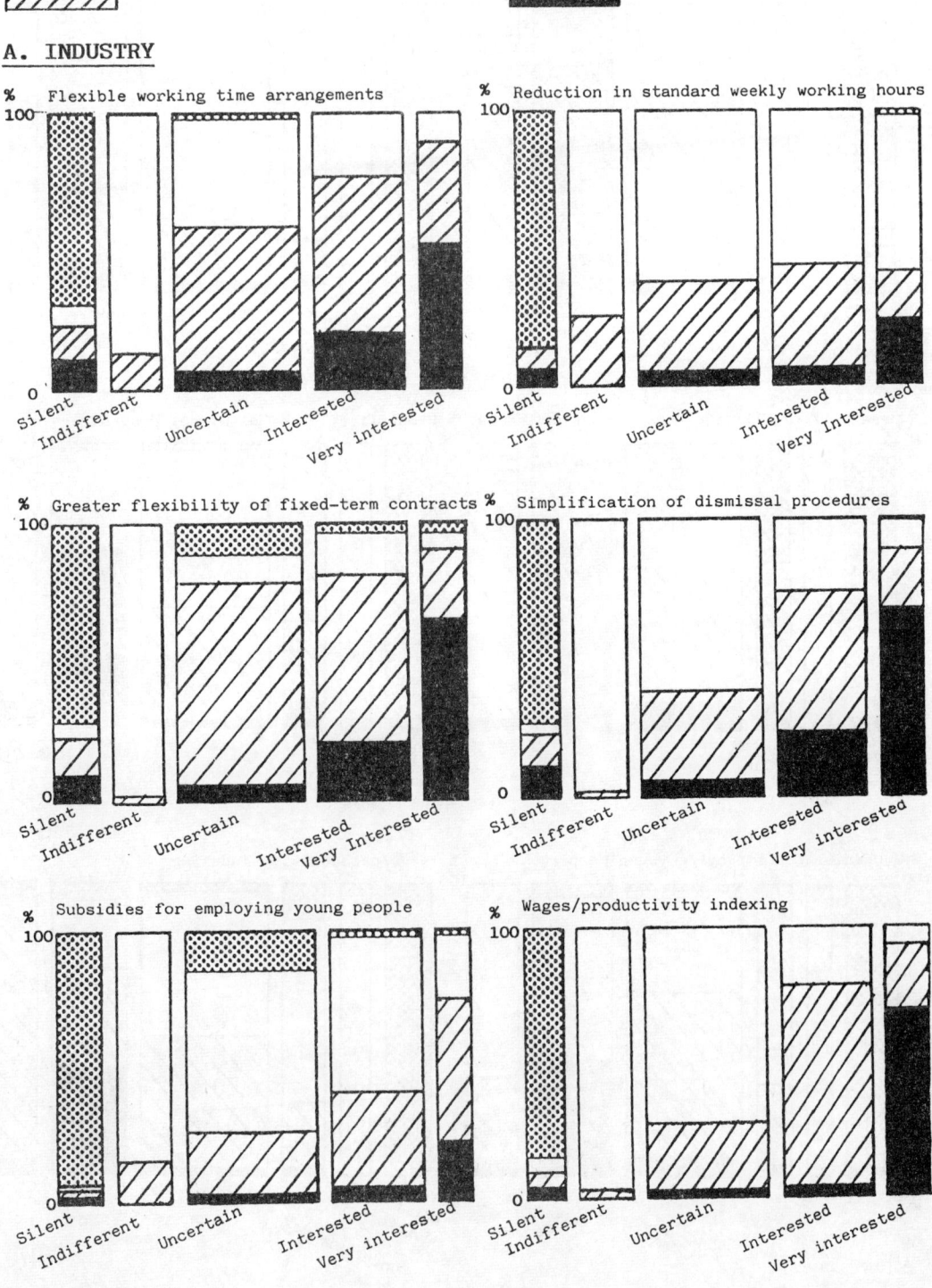

- ▦ A significant increase
- ☐ A slight increase
- ▨ No change or a decrease
- ■ No answer

A. INDUSTRY

% Flexible working time arrangements
Silent / Indifferent / Uncertain / Interested / Very interested

% Reduction in standard weekly working hours
Silent / Indifferent / Uncertain / Interested / Very Interested

% Greater flexibility of fixed-term contracts
Silent / Indifferent / Uncertain / Interested / Very Interested

% Simplification of dismissal procedures
Silent / Indifferent / Uncertain / Interested / Very interested

% Subsidies for employing young people
Silent / Indifferent / Uncertain / Interested / Very interested

% Wages/productivity indexing
Silent / Indifferent / Uncertain / Interested / Very interested

B. RETAIL TRADE

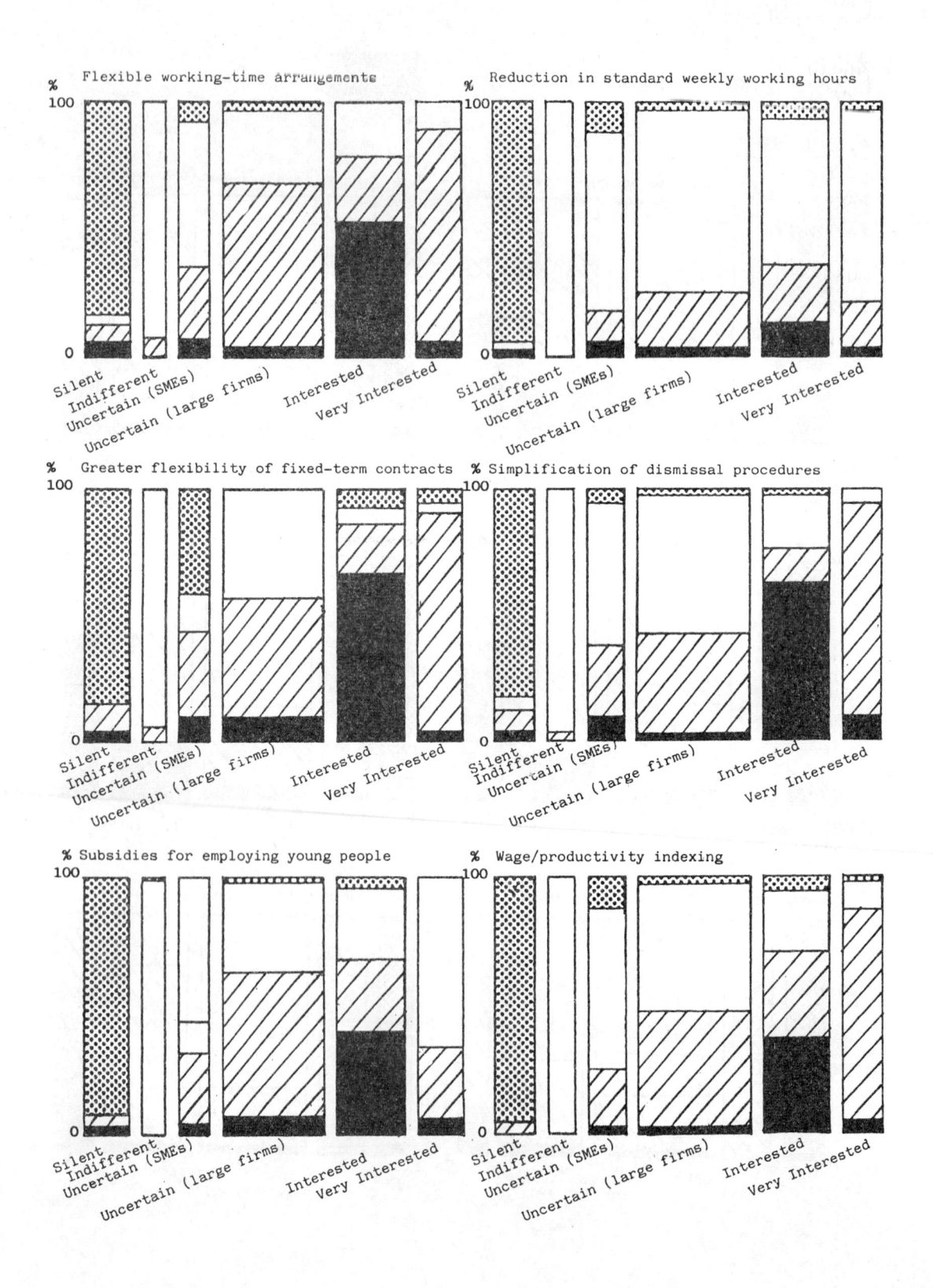

% Flexible working-time arrangements

Silent, Indifferent, Uncertain (SMEs), Uncertain (large firms), Interested, Very Interested

% Reduction in standard weekly working hours

Silent, Indifferent, Uncertain (SMEs), Uncertain (large firms), Interested, Very Interested

% Greater flexibility of fixed-term contracts

Silent, Indifferent, Uncertain (SMEs), Uncertain (large firms), Interested, Very Interested

% Simplification of dismissal procedures

Silent, Indifferent, Uncertain (SMEs), Uncertain (large firms), Interested, Very Interested

% Subsidies for employing young people

Silent, Indifferent, Uncertain (SMEs), Uncertain (large firms), Interested, Very Interested

% Wage/productivity indexing

Silent, Indifferent, Uncertain (SMEs), Uncertain (large firms), Interested, Very Interested

Such a typology clearly illustrates that, as Mireille Elbaum succinctly states, "firms expect more from flexibility when they have already introduced it", ie when they already make extensive use of fixed-term contracts and "have an optimistic view of their situation". When they are under-staffed, firms want dismissal regulations to be relaxed; when they are over-staffed, they are more in favour of flexible working time arrangements.

This detailed analysis of the survey applied to a specific country throws light on the factors at play in the formation of firms' opinions on flexibility. As we have seen, a firm's size, sector of activity and financial situation are of considerable significance. It would doubtless be possible to conduct identical analyses for all the EEC countries. Italian and, to a lesser degree, Belgian firms are strong supporters of any measure that might encourage flexibility. German firms, although they are already better catered for in this respect than their competitors, would like to see applicants better trained. Firms in Denmark, Luxembourg and the Netherlands are the most sceptical about all the measures suggested. They are prepared to introduce job-sharing but woe betide anyone who suggests they introduce a policy of wider wage differentials.

So what we have is a situation full of contrasts, with a few strong trends - but that is precisely what our analysis of the regulations suggested.

III. In conclusion: prescriptions...

It is particularly difficult to summarize a few documents chosen, perhaps somewhat arbitrarily, from an ever-increasing wealth of literature.

Some salient points do however emerge, which it _may_ be worth stressing.

Both opinion and behavioural analyses of the most successful firms indicate that it is becoming more and more difficult to persist in the most traditional method of separating company management into the distinct areas of financial and social management. Firms' success today depends on their ability to see the factors of production as an integrated whole and not as a series of subordinate relations. The workforce can no longer simply play the role of an adjustment variable. This view is not yet shared by all firms, as is illustrated by the variety of opinions held not only in the various Member States but also within any given country.

This dichotomy is also evident to a certain degree in the views of flexibility held by the social partners. This is perhaps an over-simplification, but it would seem that the trade unions are in favour of the functional flexibility of firms, provided that it is not achieved through the development of numerical flexibility; on the other hand, employers' representatives claim that the current economic situation calls for substantial numerical flexibility, which does not mean that they are against functional flexibility, particularly as regards technological change.

These positions, or prescriptions, are partly - but only partly - rooted in the political stance of the two sides. Functional flexibility is difficult to introduce and is a long and expensive process, but it does guarantee a firm's ability to adapt in the long term. By contrast, numerical flexibility allows for day-to-day survival, a sort of "contact flying" through the eye of the storm, but it will not necessarily bring firms out safely on the other side if their crew is too unstable. There is absolutely no sense in firms believing that they can manufacture products or provide services of good quality or make the best use of plant with employees who know they have no future within the firm. It is ridiculous to think that the increased precariousness of employment for a growing and very specific section of the population, particularly the young, will have no effect on their conception of work and, in a broader sense, on their view of society as a whole.

The report on the flexibility of the labour market, produced by a team of top-level experts headed by Professor Dahrendorf at the Secretariat-General of the OECD, arrives at a similar conclusion to the one reached here. This team of experts feel that "the practical problem is to discover how we can reconcile the job security that we would like to see with the necessary flexibility of the labour market".

The experts believe that this reconciliation can be achieved only through negotiation; this view, which is shared by the author of the present report, is not in this case based on any blind faith in collective bargaining, but on the observations and analyses that have been put forward here.

Only negotiation can integrate the very wide diversity of situations and opinions which are in evidence at European level. Negotiation is the only way of formulating flexible regulations which could control the possible excesses of numerical flexibility:

- part-time working must come to represent more of a freedom and less of a constraint if it is to remain an expression of solidarity;

- flexible working-time arrangements must not damage workers' health or detrimentally affect their family and social life;

- temporary contracts must not be a symbol of precarious employment for a group of individuals stigmatized by a society which is incapable of thinking of the future.

Likewise, only negotiation can take account of the elements of uncertainty inherent in functional flexibility, which is the only way of ensuring that firms can be adaptable.

Outside the European Community, the countries which have best managed to withstand unemployment when their industries have been faced with the same problems are those which have been able, by collective agreement, to find original methods of social regulation. These examples lead us to believe that the way in which the features of flexibility are defined is just as important as its content. Furthermore, the acceptability of flexibility undoubtedly depends on how it is perceived. No doubt the wider European market will rise to the occasion.

ANNEXES

BIBLIOGRAPHY

BELLOC B. "De plus en plus de salariés à temps partiel"
Economie et statistiques 193 : 1987

BLANPAIN P. Legal and contractual limitations to working time in the European Community Member States Dublin 24/25 Sept. 1987

BLOCH L., PUIG J.P. "Baisser les salaires réels, réduire les sureffectifs industriels: deux aspects de la flexibilité de l'emploi" Economie et statistiques 1986

BOISARD P., GUELAUD F. "Conséquence des horaires atypiques sur la vie quotidienne des salariés" May 1987, duplicate document.

BOYER R. (under the direction of), La flexibilité du travail en Europe Paris, la Découverte, 1986

BRINKMAN C. "Les aspects démographiques de la main d'oeuvre et de l'emploi" Conseil de l'Europe Etudes démographiques 19 : 1987

CASEY B. "The extent and nature of temporary employment in Great Britian" International conference on the changing nature of employment: new forms and areas. Sponsered by the Commission of the European Communities, Paris - June 1987

CERCOM - GERM Les jeunes face à l'emploi
European research: proceedings from a seminar held at Marseille, 24/26 Sept 1987

CHIESI A. "The organisation of time in society" Milan, feb 1985 Istituto superior di Sociologia

CORBEL P., GUERGOAT J.C., LAULHE M.C. "Les mouvements de main d'oeuvre en 1985: nouvelle progression des contrats à durée déterminée" Economie et statistiques

CORDOVA E. "De l'emploi total au travail atypique vers un virage dans l'évolution des relations de travail?" Revue Internationale du Travail vol 125-6 : 1986

DAHRENDORF R., KÖHLER E., PIOTET F. New forms of work and activity European Foundation for the Improvement of Living and Working Conditions, 1986

ELBAUM M. "L'attitude des entreprises françaises"
"Une comparaison France, Belgique, Royaume-Uni"
"Qu'attendent les entreprises de la flexibilité de l'emploi"
Economie et statistiques 197 : March 1987

European Economy 27 March, 1986

EUROSTAT 1987

FAST II: Research theme - scenarios for work. October, 1985

"Flexibilité du marché du travail" Report of a high-level group of experts to the Secretary General, Paris, O.E.C.D. 1986

"Flexibilité et emplois: mythes et réalités" 1985
"Flexibilité du temps de travail en Europe occidentale, caractéristiques, conséquences et positions syndicales" 1987 ISE

FORUM EXPO LIAISONS SOCIALES International seminar on work. Liaisons Sociales documents 127 : 1985

GIRARD A., STOETZEL J. "Les Français et les valeurs du temps présent" Revue française de sociologie XXVI 1985

GROOTING P. STEFANOV M. Transition from school to work International Sociological Association, 1984

HOLLARD. M, MARGIRIER G. "Nouveau procès de production et implication macro-économique: contribution au débat sur la flexibilité" Formation-Emploi 14 : 1986

KRAVARITOU Y. <u>New forms of work and activity, their repercussions on labour law and social security law</u> Dublin 24/25, Sept 1985

"Labour market flexibility" <u>Labour and Society, Cahiers Economiques de Bruxelles</u>, vol. 12, 1-1-87

MAURY J.M. <u>La pratique de la flexibilité de l'emploi dans les entreprises européennes de taille moyennes</u>, Nov 1986

MAURY J.M. (Study co-ordinated by) <u>La flexibilité de l'emploi dans les pays de la C.E.E.</u> Sept 1985, Travail et Société

MEAGER N. "Temporary work in Britian" <u>Employment Gazette</u> 1-86

MELLOR E., HAUGEN S. "Hourly paid workers: who they are and what they earn" <u>Monthly Labor Review</u>, Feb 1986

NARDONE T. "Part-time workers: who are they?" <u>Monthly Labour Review</u> Feb 1986

NEUBOURG C. "Le travail à temps partiel: comparaison quantitative internationale" <u>Revue Internationale du Travail</u> Sept 1987

"Perspectives de l'emploi" O.E.C.D. Sept 1987

PIORE M. "Outline for a research agenda for the new industrial organization" (duplicate document 25p. 1987)

STANDING G. "La flexibilité du travail et la marginalisation des travailleurs âgés" <u>Revue internationale du travail</u> May-June 1986

SARFATI H., KOBRIN C. <u>La flexibilité du marché de l'emploi, un enjeu économique et social</u> B.I.T. Genève 1987

STANKIEWICZ F. "Flexibilité courante et flexibilité structurelle" LAST 1986

STOETZEL J. <u>Les valeurs du temps présent</u>, Paris P.U.F. 1983

STAINES G., PLECK J. "nonstandard work schedules and family life" Journal of applied psychology, vol 69-3 : 1984

VOGEL-POLSKY E. "les nouvelles formes de travail" Oct 1986 (duplicate document 46p.)

VOIRIN M. "La réduction de la durée du travail et la sécurité sociale" Colloquim on trends in working time in the countries of Western Europe: reductions in working time. Genève, 11/13 Feb 1986

QUESTIONNAIRE FOR WAGE EARNERS

Table 1

Increase in pay or shorter working time preferred?

Question: If the choice were offered at the next wage round, which of the following possibilities would you prefer?
1. Increase in pay, for the same hours of work as now
2. No increase in pay but shorter working time
? Don't know

	1	2	?	Total
Community level (EUR 10)				
Total of all employees	61	31	8	100
Sex				
— Men	62	31	7	100
— Women	60	31	9	100
Age (years)				
— Under 25	67	28	5	100
— 25-39	59	34	7	100
— 40-54	62	31	7	100
— 55 and older	59	25	16	100
Family income (income pyramid)				
— Lower quartile	62	22	16	100
— Second quartile	65	29	6	100
— Third quartile	64	30	6	100
— Upper quartile	56	39	5	100
Function				
— Manual worker	66	29	5	100
— White collar/office worker	59	34	7	100
— Executive/top management	62	30	8	100
Union membership				
— Active member	62	32	6	100
— Only paying member	60	34	6	100
— Not member but sympathetic	61	32	7	100
— Not member and not interested	62	30	8	100
Weekly working time (hours)				
— Less than 25	69	24	7	100
— 25-34	67	24	9	100
— 35-40	59	37	4	100
— 41 and more	68	27	5	100
Sector				
— Public	61	33	6	100
— Private	61	30	9	100
Member countries				
— Belgium	58	36	6	100
— Denmark	38	51	11	100
— FR of Germany	56	30	14	100
— Greece	68	26	6	100
— Spain	64	31	5	100
— France	62	34	4	100
— Ireland	78	19	3	100
— Italy	55	39	6	100
— Luxembourg	58	36	6	100
— The Netherlands	46	47	7	100
— Portugal	82	11	7	100
— United Kingdom	77	19	4	100
European Community (EUR 12)	62	30	8	100

Source: EC employee survey 1985 86.

Table 2

Present and desired working time

Question: 1. what is your present working time per week?
2. You sometimes hear that not everyone is fully satisfied with his/her current working time. Assuming that the present hourly wage rate remained unchanged how many hours per week would you like to work?

(Answers in %)

		less than 20 h	20 to 24 h	25 to 29 h	30 to 34 h	35 to 40 h	41 to 44 h	45 and more	No answer	Total
Community level (EUR 10)										
Total of all employees	1 (actual)	7.5	4.8	2.8	3.8	55.0	12.4	10.2	3.4	100.0
	2 (ideal)	7.7	4.9	4.8	17.5	48.3	6.3	3.7	6.6	100.0
Sex										
— Men	1 (actual)	1.5	1.3	0.7	2.8	61.6	16.3	13.4	2.4	100.0
	2 (ideal)	1.8	1.6	3.3	17.6	56.3	8.0	5.3	6.1	100.0
— Women	1 (actual)	17.0	10.3	6.3	5.5	44.5	6.3	5.0	5.1	100.0
	2 (ideal)	17.2	10.3	7.4	17.3	33.5	3.5	1.2	7.6	100.0
Age (years)										
— Under 25	1 (actual)	4.7	3.1	2.4	4.0	61.1	11.5	10.8	2.4	100.0
	2 (ideal)	2.1	3.1	4.2	18.6	51.8	7.3	7.2	5.7	100.0
— 25-39	1 (actual)	8.5	4.7	2.2	4.6	54.7	13.4	9.9	2.1	100.0
	2 (ideal)	8.7	4.8	4.8	19.8	47.3	6.2	2.8	5.6	100.0
— 40-54	1 (actual)	6.9	5.9	3.5	3.0	55.5	13.0	8.7	3.5	100.0
	2 (ideal)	7.9	6.0	5.3	16.2	49.8	5.9	3.4	5.6	100.0
— 55 and older	1 (actual)	9.7	4.2	4.1	2.7	46.2	8.1	14.9	10.1	100.0
	2 (ideal)	11.5	4.7	4.7	10.1	43.1	6.8	3.9	15.2	100.0
Family income (income pyramid)										
— Lower quartile	1 (actual)	2.9	8.1	3.0	2.4	52.1	12.7	6.0	12.8	100.0
	2 (ideal)	6.7	3.5	5.8	9.4	53.7	7.7	0.8	12.4	100.0
— Second quartile	1 (actual)	7.1	3.6	2.1	2.7	62.7	13.4	5.7	2.7	100.0
	2 (ideal)	7.2	4.5	4.6	17.5	52.7	6.1	1.5	5.9	100.0
— Third quartile	1 (actual)	7.0	4.7	2.8	3.8	59.0	11.0	10.3	1.4	100.0
	2 (ideal)	7.2	5.2	4.5	17.3	50.0	7.2	4.9	3.7	100.0
— Upper quartile	1 (actual)	6.1	4.0	3.2	5.0	54.1	12.8	13.5	1.3	100.0
	2 (ideal)	8.4	5.3	4.4	22.1	45.8	5.3	4.2	4.5	100.0
Function										
— Manual worker	1 (actual)	8.6	4.3	2.4	2.3	58.5	13.3	8.7	2.0	100.0
	2 (ideal)	7.2	4.8	3.8	15.9	53.4	7.0	3.8	4.0	100.0
— White collar/office worker	1 (actual)	7.4	5.3	3.5	5.0	57.3	11.0	7.9	2.9	100.0
	2 (ideal)	9.0	5.4	6.0	19.6	46.3	5.2	2.4	6.1	100.0
— Executive/top management	1 (actual)	4.3	2.4	1.0	4.1	42.9	17.8	23.4	2.1	100.0
	2 (ideal)	4.6	3.3	3.2	19.1	41.7	8.4	11.1	8.6	100.0
Union membership										
— Active member	1 (actual)	2.5	1.4	2.6	3.2	66.5	13.7	8.8	1.3	100.0
	2 (ideal)	3.5	1.6	5.1	24.6	51.0	4.9	5.6	3.7	100.0
— Only paying member	1 (actual)	4.4	3.3	3.3	6.1	62.2	12.7	7.4	0.6	100.0
	2 (ideal)	4.3	5.4	6.8	18.5	50.8	5.7	3.7	4.8	100.0

Table 2 *(continued)*

		\multicolumn{8}{c}{Weekly working hours}	
		less than 20 h	20 to 24 h	25 to 29 h	30 to 34 h	35 to 40 h	41 to 44 h	45 and more	No answer	Total
— Not member but sympathetic	1 (actual)	9,5	6,1	1,9	3,2	53,1	12,3	10,1	3,8	100,0
	2 (ideal)	8,9	5,2	4,5	15,9	52,0	5,1	2,0	6,4	100,0
— Not member and not interested	1 (actual)	10,0	5,5	2,9	3,0	49.0	12,5	12,1	5,0	100,0
	2 (ideal)	10,8	5,5	3,7	16,8	43,8	8,1	4,4	6,9	100,0
Weekly working time (hours)										
— Less than 25	1 (actual)	61,3	38,7	—	—	—	—	—	—	100,0
	2 (ideal)	50,7	24,4	4,4	2,8	13,2	0,5	1,6	2,4	100,0
— 25-34	1 (actual)	—	—	42,5	57,5	—	—	—	—	100,0
	2 (ideal)	8,8	12,7	27,9	35,0	9,9	0,2	—	5,5	100,0
— 35-40	1 (actual)	—	—	—	—	100.0	—	—	—	—
	2 (ideal)	1,2	1,8	4,0	22,7	63,5	2,4	1,1	3,3	100,0
— 41 and more	1 (actual)	—	—	—	—	—	55,0	45,0	—	100,0
	2 (ideal)	0,8	0,4	1,0	9,8	46,7	21,8	13,1	6,4	100,0
Sector										
— Public	1 (actual)	8.9	5.1	4.5	6.2	57,6	8.5	7.6	1.6	100.0
	2 (ideal)	9,6	6,9	6,4	19,5	45,6	4,3	3,0	4,7	100,0
— Private	1 (actual)	6,8	4,6	2,0	2,6	53,6	14,5	11,5	4,4	100,0
	2 (ideal)	6,8	3,9	4,1	16,4	49,8	7,4	4,1	7,5	100,0
Member countries										
— Belgium	1 (actual)	6.0	6.2	1.8	5.2	68.3	5.7	5.7	1.0	100.0
	2 (ideal)	6,2	5,5	7,3	22,6	46,5	4,7	1,8	5,5	100,0
— Denmark	1 (actual)	4,4	5,7	5,7	5,1	60,5	5,4	9,5	3,8	100,0
	2 (ideal)	3,5	5,9	5,6	18,9	51,5	4,1	3,0	7,4	100,0
— FR of Germany	1 (actual)	3,8	3,5	2,2	2,3	54,0	18,4	6,8	8,9	100,0
	2 (ideal)	4,7	2,2	1,8	13,9	54,9	8,1	2,2	12,0	100,0
— Greece	1 (actual)	2,1	1,6	5,3	4,3	64,4	10,6	9,6	2,1	100,0
	2 (ideal)	2,1	4,3	8,5	20,7	54,3	3,7	2,1	4,3	100,0
— Spain	1 (actual)	1,9	0,5	3,0	6,0	53,5	18,3	16,2	0,6	100,0
	2 (ideal)	4,4	3,0	5,6	13,9	55,2	8,5	4,5	4,9	100,0
— France	1 (actual)	5,2	5,8	2,6	3,5	60,8	12,4	8,5	1,3	100,0
	2 (ideal)	3,8	5,6	3,6	17,6	53,2	7,8	3,7	4,8	100,0
— Ireland	1 (actual)	4,0	1,4	2,2	5,0	62,9	15,1	9,0	0,4	100,0
	2 (ideal)	4,7	3,2	3,2	20,1	56,1	5,4	4,7	2,5	100,0
— Italy	1 (actual)	5,3	4,3	2,2	4,6	56,3	10,2	14,9	2,2	100,0
	2 (ideal)	6,8	5,6	9,0	24,5	43,0	4,3	3,1	3,7	100,0
— Luxembourg	1 (actual)	2,8	6,5	1,9	1,9	65,4	14,0	7,5	—	100,0
	2 (ideal)	1,9	8,4	1,9	8,4	66,4	6,5	2,8	3,7	100,0
— The Netherlands	1 (actual)	11,2	5,3	2,7	4,9	53,4	6,3	12,2	4,0	100,0
	2 (ideal)	9,7	9,5	3,6	12,4	48,4	4,2	5,6	6,6	100,0
— Portugal	1 (actual)	1,8	2,7	2,5	4,1	34,1	26,6	24,2	4,0	100,0
	2 (ideal)	1,9	3,0	4,1	16,8	42,6	19,5	3,7	8,4	100,0
— United Kingdom	1 (actual)	15,3	5,4	3,8	4,5	47,2	10,8	12,2	0,6	100,0
	2 (ideal)	15,6	5,7	5,7	16,2	40,2	5,8	6,0	4,8	100,0
European Community (EUR 12)	1 (actual)	6,7	4,3	2,8	4,0	54,2	13,5	11,3	3,1	100,0
	2 (ideal)	7,2	4,6	4,9	17,1	48,9	6,9	3,8	6,5	100,0

Source: EC employee survey 1985/86.

Table 3

Actual and preferred working time (micro analysis; EUR 10)

(Answers in %)

Whole of wage-earners	Actual working time (weekly hours)						
	Less than 20	20-24	25-29	30-34	35-40	41-45	More than 45
Ideal working time (weekly hours)							
— Less than 20	74	14	13	6	1	—	1
— 20-24	3	58	20	7	2	1	1
— 25-29	5	4	44	16	4	2	—
— 30-34	3	2	5	57	23	12	7
— 35-40	12	15	9	10	63	50	42
— 41-45	0	1	0	0	2	28	14
— More than 45	0	3	0	0	1	3	26
— No answer	3	3	9	4	4	4	9
Total	100	100	100	100	100	100	100
(% share of this category of actual working time)	(7.5)	(4,8)	(2.8)	(3.8)	(55.0)	(12,4)	(10,2)

Men	Actual working time (weekly hours)						
	Less than 20	20-24	25-29	30-34	35-40	41-45	More than 45
Ideal working time (weekly hours)							
— Less than 20	73	20	—	4	—	1	—
— 20-24	1	51	2	7	1	—	—
— 25-29	4	—	72	13	4	1	—
— 30-34	9	28	19	60	21	12	7
— 35-40	—	1	2	14	67	51	41
— 41-45	1	—	—	1	3	27	14
— More than 45	4	—	—	—	1	3	29
— No answer	8	—	5	1	3	5	9
Total	100	100	100	100	100	100	100
(% share of this category[1] of actual working time)	(1,6)	(1,3)	(0,7)	(2,7)	(61,6)	(16,3)	(13,4)

Women	Actual working time (weekly hours)						
	Less than 20	20-24	25-29	30-34	35-40	41-45	More than 45
Ideal working time (weekly hours)							
— Less than 20	74	13	15	7	3	—	5
— 20-24	3	59	24	7	3	2	1
— 25-29	5	5	40	18	6	2	—
— 30-34	2	3	3	55	27	13	8
— 35-40	14	12	10	8	56	50	47
— 41-45	—	1	—	—	2	32	12
— More than 45	—	4	—	—	—	—	13
— No answer	2	3	8	5	3	1	13
Total	100	100	100	100	100	100	100
(% share of this category[1] of actual working time)	(16,9)	(10,2)	(6,4)	(5,6)	(44,5)	(6,4)	(5,0)

[1] The figures do not add up exactly to 100%, as between 2 and 5% of interviewed persons did not specify their present working time.
Source: EC employee survey 1985 86

Table 4

Flexible working time

Question: Let us assume that more flexible working time arrangements will be offered in the near future. Which one would you prefer assuming that the salary is the same?
  1. Same working hours every day
  2. Fixed amount of working hours per month but the number of working days and working hours per day could be agreed on according to production and/or work organization requirements
  3. Fixed amount of working hours per year but with periods of hard work which would involve long hours and other periods of shorter hours or holidays according to production and/or work organization requirements
  ? Don't know

(Answers in %)

	1	2	3	?	Total
Community level (EUR 10)					
Total of all employees	38	39	16	7	100
Sex					
— Men	37	38	18	7	100
— Women	38	41	13	8	100
Age (years)					
— Under 25	39	42	15	4	100
— 25-39	36	41	18	5	100
— 40-54	37	41	14	8	100
— 55 and older	46	23	16	15	100
Family income (income pyramid)					
— Lower quartile	36	33	17	14	100
— Second quartile	42	35	14	9	100
— Third quartile	39	42	14	5	100
— Upper quartile	31	43	23	3	100
Function					
— Manual worker	42	37	14	7	100
— White collar/office worker	35	41	18	6	100
— Executive/top management	30	43	21	6	100
Union membership					
— Active member	38	43	16	3	100
— Only paying member	42	37	17	4	100
— Not member but sympathetic	32	43	16	9	100
— Not member and not interested	39	36	17	8	100
Weekly working time (hours)					
— Less than 25	44	40	8	8	100
— 25-34	40	32	18	10	100
— 35-40	42	40	14	4	100
— 41 and more	27	42	25	6	100
Sector					
— Public	37	41	17	5	100
— Private	38	38	16	8	100

Table 5

New working time arrangements

Question: Supposing you were offered the following working time arrangements:

You work for example one Saturday a month, or else you work five times a month up to 22.00 in the evening, and as a counterpart, your working time per year is reduced by 5% (that could be 2 hours less work per week in the average or else it could be two weeks more vacation a year).

What is your personal opinion on such an arrangement?

Are you 1. very much in favour
2. rather in favour
3. rather against
4. very much against
5. indifferent
? Don't know

	1	2	3	4	5	?	Total
Community level (EUR 10)							
Total of all Employees	12	26	20	14	18	10	100
Sex							
— Men	14	26	19	13	19	9	100
— Women	11	25	21	15	16	12	100
Age (years)							
— Under 25	13	29	21	11	19	7	100
— 25-39	13	28	20	14	16	9	100
— 40-54	10	23	20	16	20	11	100
— 55 and older	10	19	14	15	20	22	100
Family income (income pyramid)							
— Lower quartile	10	24	16	12	18	20	100
— Second quartile	11	26	18	16	19	10	100
— Third quartile	11	27	20	15	19	8	100
— Upper quartile	17	25	20	13	18	7	100
Function							
— Manual worker	14	24	20	14	19	9	100
— White collar/office worker	12	28	19	15	17	9	100
— Executive/top management	12	27	16	13	23	9	100
Union membership							
— Active member	12	24	22	17	17	8	100
— Only paying member	14	25	19	17	17	8	100
— Not member but sympathetic	11	27	18	11	22	11	100
— Not member and not interested	12	26	20	14	17	11	100
Weekly working time (hours)							
— Less than 25	11	27	18	17	17	10	100
— 25-34	12	25	19	13	22	9	100
— 35-40	12	26	22	15	18	7	100
— 41 and more	14	27	17	12	20	10	100
Sector							
— Public	13	26	18	15	18	10	100
— Private	12	26	20	14	18	10	100
Member countries							
— Belgium	15	19	29	18	12	7	100
— Denmark	11	19	14	20	16	20	100
— FR of Germany	8	28	17	9	24	14	100
— Greece	26	20	12	18	15	9	100
— Spain	12	28	20	13	18	9	100
— France	14	33	23	13	13	4	100
— Ireland	25	28	11	12	13	11	100
— Italy	14	25	20	18	11	12	100
— Luxembourg	10	26	20	19	16	9	100
— The Netherlands	12	20	19	29	12	8	100
— Portugal	12	31	16	2	25	14	100
— United Kingdom	13	21	18	13	25	10	100
European Community (EUR 12)	12	26	20	14	18	10	100

Source: EC employee survey 1985 86.

Table 6

Connection between readiness to evening and Saturday work and preferred changes in daily working hours (micro analysis; EUR 10)

(Answers in %)

In favour of:	For or against more flexible working hours	For or against more flexible organization of working time including evening and Saturday work			Total	
		For	Against	Indifferent/ no answer		
— same hours every day		28	44	28	100	(38%)[1]
— fixed amount of working hours per month but the number of working days and working hours per day could be agreed on according to production and/or work organization requirements		46	31	23	100	(39%)[1]
— fixed amount of working hours per year but with periods of hard work which would involve long hours and other periods of shorter hours or holidays according to production and/or work organization requirements		55	23	22	100	(23%)[1]

[1] % share of this category.
Example how to read the figures in the table: Of the respondents in favour of same hours every day (38% of all employees interviewed) 28% are for more flexible organization of working time including evening and Saturday work.
Source EC employee survey 1985/86.

Table 7

Solidarity with company in bad times

Question: In some countries salaried people are accepting lower salaries when their company is in difficulty, with the understanding that when the company will do better, they will get a share of the profits.

What is your personal opinion on such arrangements?

Are you 1. very much in favour
2. rather in favour
3. rather against
4. very much against
5. indifferent
? Don't know

	1	2	3	4	5	?	Total
Community level (EUR 10)							
Total of all Employees	18	33	18	11	14	6	100
Sex							
— Men	18	31	19	13	13	6	100
— Women	17	37	16	8	14	8	100
Age (years)							
— Under 25	16	32	19	13	16	4	100
— 25-39	19	36	19	11	11	4	100
— 40-54	16	34	18	9	15	8	100
— 55 and older	19	23	12	10	20	16	100
Family income (income pyramid)							
— Lower quartile	23	27	15	8	14	13	100
— Second quartile	15	32	21	13	10	9	100
— Third quartile	17	37	14	12	16	4	100
— Upper quartile	21	36	18	9	13	3	100
Function							
— Manual worker	19	31	18	13	14	5	100
— White collar/office worker	17	35	19	10	14	5	100
— Executive/top management	18	40	13	9	12	8	100
Union membership							
— Active member	18	31	17	19	11	4	100
— Only paying member	18	30	20	15	13	4	100
— Not member but sympathetic	15	37	17	8	16	7	100
— Not member and not interested	20	34	17	8	14	7	100
Weekly working time (hours)							
— Less than 25	22	42	14	4	12	6	100
— 25-34	18	36	16	14	14	2	100
— 35-40	16	33	20	12	15	4	100
— 41 and more	21	33	16	12	13	5	100
Sector							
— Public	17	35	17	12	14	5	100
— Private	18	33	18	10	14	7	100

Table 8

Bonus or profit-sharing

Question: In 1984, did you personally get some bonus or profit-sharing because of the performance of the company you work with? If yes, how much approximately was this bonus or profit-sharing? The equivalent of one week of salary, one month of salary?

	Nothing	Less than 1 month salary	1 month's or more	Not been working in 1984 or no answer	Total
Community level (EUR 10)					
Total of all employees	77	10	6	7	100
Sex					
— Men	76	11	8	5	100
— Women	78	9	4	9	•100
Age (years)					
— Under 25	76	14	5	5	100
— 25-39	79	10	6	5	100
— 40-54	77	9	8	6	100
— 55 and older	72	8	6	14	100
Family income (income pyramid)					
— Lower quartile	78	7	3	12	100
— Second quartile	78	10	5	7	100
— Third quartile	77	12	6	5	100
— Upper quartile	78	9	10	3	100
Function					
— Manual Worker	77	12	5	6	100
— White collar/office worker	79	9	7	5	100
— Executive/top management	65	10	20	5	100
Union membership					
— Active member	78	9	8	5	100
— Only paying member	79	12	6	3	100
— Not member but sympathetic	77	8	6	9	100
— Not member and not interested	76	10	7	7	100
Weekly working time (hours)					
— Less than 25	85	7	2	6	100
— 25-34	86	8	2	4	100
— 35-40	79	12	6	3	100
— 41 and more	71	10	12	7	100
Sector					
— Public	89	4	4	3	100
— Private	71	13	8	8	100
Member countries:					
— Belgium	81	11	5	3	100
— Denmark	87	3	2	8	100
— FR of Germany	79	4	6	11	100
— Greece	76	9	4	11	100
— Spain	71	7	7	15	100
— France	71	14	10	5	100
— Ireland	77	10	6	7	100
— Italy	85	8	2	5	100
— Luxembourg	69	10	18	3	100
— The Netherlands	77	8	12	3	100
— Portugal	84	5	5	6	100
— United Kingdom	73	16	8	3	100
European Community (EUR 12)	77	10	6	7	100

Source: EC employee survey 1985/86.

Table 9

Salaries according to personal efficiency

Question: In some places, individual salaries for the same job are different according to the personal efficiency at work of the people. What is your opinion on such an arrangement?

Are you 1. very much in favour
2. rather in favour
3. rather against
4. very much against
5. indifferent
? Don't know

	1	2	3	4	5	?	Total
Community level (EUR 10)							
Total of all Employees	24	32	16	11	11	6	100
Sex							
— Men	26	31	16	11	11	5	100
— Women	21	34	17	12	9	7	100
Age (years)							
— Under 25	22	33	16	13	12	4	100
— 25-39	25	32	17	13	9	4	100
— 40-54	22	32	18	10	12	6	100
— 55 and older	30	29	11	8	8	14	100
Family income (income pyramid)							
— Lower quartile	18	31	18	10	13	10	100
— Second quartile	18	34	16	11	14	7	100
— Third quartile	24	32	16	13	10	5	100
— Upper quartile	31	32	16	11	8	2	100
Function							
— Manual worker	23	29	19	13	12	4	100
— White collar/office worker	23	34	16	12	10	5	100
— Executive/top management	45	30	9	7	5	4	100
Union membership							
— Active member	21	31	19	17	8	4	100
— Only paying member	25	28	17	14	12	4	100
— Not member but sympathetic	21	34	17	10	12	6	100
— Not member and not interested	28	33	15	10	8	6	100
Weekly working time (hours)							
— Less than 25	22	37	16	10	10	5	100
— 25-34	27	27	15	14	13	4	100
— 35-40	23	32	18	12	12	3	100
— 41 and more	31	32	15	10	8	4	100
Sector							
— Public	24	32	19	12	9	4	100
— Private	24	32	15	11	11	7	100
Member countries							
— Belgium	17	26	27	12	13	5	100
— Denmark	25	20	11	26	8	10	100
— FR of Germany	17	33	13	10	19	8	100
— Greece	36	26	13	12	5	8	100
— Spain	26	31	15	15	7	6	100
— France	24	37	20	11	6	2	100
— Ireland	31	32	15	8	8	6	100
— Italy	27	34	18	11	4	6	100
— Luxembourg	30	24	14	21	8	3	100
— Netherlands	20	41	13	18	4	4	100
— Portugal	10	43	19	5	16	7	100
— United Kingdom	32	26	16	11	11	4	100
European Community (EUR 12)	24	32	16	11	11	6	100

Source: EC employee survey 1985/86.

Table 10

Connection between interest in payment related to profits and/or losses and to performance (micro analysis; EUR 10)

(Answers in %)

For or against a temporary reduction in pay if the employee's company is in difficulty (provided that the employee later shares in the profits when the firm is doing better again)	For or against wages or salary being in accordance with personal performance				
	In favour	Against	Undecided/ no answer		Total
— Very much in favour	71	23	6	100	(18%)[1]
— Rather in favour	59	27	14	100	(33%)[1]
— Rather against	51	35	14	100	(18%)[1]
— Very much against	43	46	10	100	(11%)[1]
Total	46	27	17	100	(100%)

[1] % share of this category; the figures do not add up to 100% because 20% of the respondents had no definite opinion.
How to read the table (example): of the respondents very much in favour of profit and loss sharing (18% of total employees) 71% are also in favour of payment by personal performance.
Source: EC employee survey 1985/86.

Table 12

Connection between assessment of wage differentials and general interest in payment by performance (micro-analysis; EUR 10)

(Answers in %)

% assess the differences in payment where they work to be	Amongst employees who are in favour of payment by performance...		
	Total (56%)[1]	Public sector (56%)[1]	Private sector (56%)[1]
— Fully sufficient	15 ⎫ 41	12 ⎫ 33	16 ⎫ 44
— More or less sufficient	26 ⎭	21 ⎭	28 ⎭
— Not sufficient	33	38	30
— Other response	13	17	12
— No answer	13	12	14
	100	100	100

[1] % share of employees in favour of payment by performance in this category.
How to read the figures in the table (example): Of all respondents in favour of payment by performance (56% in total) 15% assess the differences in payment at the place where they work to be fully sufficient.
Source: EC employee survey 1985/86.

Table 11

Wage differences at place of work

Question: At your place of work, would you say that the differences in pay between people who are more efficient and the other people are:
1. fully sufficient
2. more or less sufficient
3. not sufficient
4. other answer (volunteered)
? Don't know

	1	2	3	4	?	Total
Community level (EUR 10)						
Total of all employees	16	25	26	15	18	100
Sex						
— Men	16	27	28	14	15	100
— Women	15	22	24	17	22	100
Age (years)						
— Under 25	16	24	23	17	20	100
— 25-39	17	25	28	15	15	100
— 40-54	17	27	25	14	17	100
— 55 and other	8	18	28	18	28	100
Family income (income pyramid)						
— Lower quartile	13	27	25	11	24	100
— Second quartile	15	24	24	18	19	100
— Third quartile	15	26	28	16	15	100
— Upper quartile	18	26	29	14	13	100
Function						
— Manual worker	16	25	26	14	19	100
— White collar/office worker	15	26	27	16	16	100
— Executive/top management	25	24	30	12	9	100
Union membership						
— Active member	14	25	29	16	16	100
— Only paying member	21	20	26	17	16	100
— Not member but sympathetic	15	25	25	16	19	100
— Not member and not interested	13	28	28	14	17	100
Weekly working time (hours)						
— Less than 25	14	22	19	22	23	100
— 25-34	14	18	30	15	23	100
— 35-40	16	26	30	15	13	100
— 41 and more	18	28	25	15	14	100
Sector						
— Public	16	21	29	19	15	100
— Private	15	27	25	13	20	100
Member countries						
— Belgium	25	33	18	10	14	100
— Denmark	28	13	14	19	26	100
— FR of Germany	17	30	23	9	21	100
— Greece	32	22	26	3	17	100
— Spain	18	23	29	12	12	100
— France	18	20	33	16	13	100
— Ireland	15	28	18	12	27	100
— Italy	6	24	26	28	16	100
— Luxembourg	28	18	22	20	12	100
— Netherlands	26	29	23	10	12	100
— Portugal	13	29	20	1	37	100
— United Kingdom	13	23	28	15	21	100
European Community (EUR 12)	16	25	26	14	19	100

Source: EC employee survey 1985 86.

Table 13

Survey results of unemployed, European Community (EUR 12)

Questions:

	Total of all employees	Unemployed
You sometimes hear that not everyone is fully satisfied with his/her current working time. Assuming that the present hourly wage rate remained unchanged, how many hours per week would you like to work?		
— Less than 30 hours	17	13
— 30-34 hours	17	15
— 35 hours and more	60	57
— Indifferent	6	15
	100	100
Let us assume that more flexible working time arrangements will be offered in the near future. Which one would you prefer (assuming that the salary is the same)?		
Same working hours every day	40	41
Fixed amount of working hours per month but the number of working days and working hours per day could be agreed according to production and/or work organization requirements	38 ⎱ 53	35 ⎱ 49
Fixed amount of working hours per year but with periods of hard work which would involve long hours and other periods of shorter hours or holidays according to production and/or work organization requirements	15 ⎰	14 ⎰
Indifferent, don't know	7	10
	100	100
Supposing you were offered the following working time arrangements: You work for example one Saturday a month, or else you work five times a month up to 22.00 in the evening, and as a counterpart, your working time per year is reduced by 5% (that could be 2 hours less work per week in the average or else it could be two weeks more vacation a year) What is your personal opinion of such arrangements? Are you...		
— very much in favour	12 ⎱ 38	13 ⎱ 43
— rather in favour	26 ⎰	30 ⎰
— rather against	20 ⎱ 34	15 ⎱ 25
— very much against	14 ⎰	10 ⎰
— indifferent	18	14
— don't know	10	18
	100	100
In some countries salaried people are accepting to get lower salaries when their company is in difficulty, with the understanding that when the company will do better, they will get a share of the profits. What is your personal opinion of such arrangements? Are you...		
— very much in favour	18 ⎱ 51	13 ⎱ 44
— rather in favour	33 ⎰	31 ⎰
— rather against	18 ⎱ 29	16 ⎱ 27
— very much against	11 ⎰	11 ⎰
— indifferent	14	13
— don't know	6	16
	100	100
In some places, individual salaries for the same job are different according to the personal efficiency at work of the people. What is your opinion of such arrangements? Are you...		
— very much in favour	24 ⎱ 56	20 ⎱ 48
— rather in favour	32 ⎰	28 ⎰
— rather against	16 ⎱ 27	15 ⎱ 29
— very much against	11 ⎰	14 ⎰
— indifferent	11	9
— don't know	6	14
	100	100

Source: EC employee survey 1985/86.

Table 14

Survey results of students, European Community (EUR 12)
Questions:

	Total of all employees	Employees younger than 25 years	Students (15-24 years)
Let us assume that more flexible working time arrangements will be offered in the near future. Which one would you prefer (assuming that the salary is the same)?			
Same working hours every day	40	39	27
Fixed amount of working hours per month but the number of working days and working hours per day could be agreed according to production and/or work organization requirements	38 ⎫ 53	41 ⎫ 56	45 ⎫ 62
Fixed amount of working hours per year but with periods of hard work which would involve long hours and other periods of shorter hours or holidays according to production and/or work organization requirements	15 ⎭	15 ⎭	17 ⎭
Don't know	7	5	11
	100	100	100

Supposing you were offered the following working time arrangements:
You work for example one Saturday a month, or else you work five times a month up to 22.00 in the evening, and as a counterpart, your working time per year is reduced by 5% (that could be 2 hours less work per week in the average or else it could be two weeks more vacation a year) (Show card)
What is your personal opinion of such arrangements. Are you...

— very much in favour	12 ⎫ 38	13 ⎫ 42	11 ⎫ 44
— rather in favour	26 ⎭	29 ⎭	33 ⎭
— rather against	20 ⎫ 34	20 ⎫ 31	17 ⎫ 26
— very much against	14 ⎭	11 ⎭	9 ⎭
— indifferent	18	19	17
— don't know	10	8	13
	100	100	100

In some countries salaried people are accepting to get lower salaries when their company is in difficulty, with the understanding that when the company will do better, they will get a share of the profits.
What is your personal opinion of such arrangements. Are you...

— very much in favour	18 ⎫ 51	16 ⎫ 49	11 ⎫ 46
— rather in favour	33 ⎭	33 ⎭	35 ⎭
— rather against	18 ⎫ 29	18 ⎫ 30	16 ⎫ 24
— very much against	11 ⎭	12 ⎭	8 ⎭
— indifferent	14	16	17
— don't know	6	5	13
	100	100	100

In some places, individual salaries for the same job are different according to the personal efficiency at work of the people. What is your opinion of such arrangements?

— very much in favour	24 ⎫ 56	22 ⎫ 56	21 ⎫ 53
— rather in favour	32 ⎭	34 ⎭	32 ⎭
— rather against	16 ⎫ 27	15 ⎫ 29	17 ⎫ 27
— very much against	11 ⎭	14 ⎭	10 ⎭
— indifferent	11	11	8
— don't know	6	4	12
	100	100	100

**QUESTIONNAIRE FOR INDUSTRIAL COMPANIES
ACCORDING TO SECTOR AND SIZE**

Table 39*

Assessment of staff size in manufacturing industry by branch and company size class at Community level[1]

Question: In relation to each category of worker you employ, could you say whether the present number of workers in that category is larger than you really need—in relation to current and expected levels of demand—about right or smaller than you need?

(answers in %)

	Branch			Size class (employees)				All sizes
	Intermediate goods	Investment goods	Consumer goods	Less than 200	200–499	500–1 000	More than 1 000	
Skilled manual workers								
..larger	17.2	13.5	20.8	8.9	11.6	16.2	23.0	17.4
..about right	60.9	53.6	59.0	65.3	62.2	61.1	47.5	56.6
..smaller	18.0	30.0	16.2	21.4	22.2	21.1	26.3	22.1
..No answer	3.9	2.9	4.0	4.4	4.0	1.6	3.2	3.9
	100.0	100.0	100.0	100.0	100.0	100.0	100.0	100.0
Balance[2]	−0.9	−16.5	4.5	−12.4	−10.5	−4.9	−3.2	−4.7
Unskilled manual workers								
..larger	42.2	26.2	39.3	22.7	28.7	30.2	43.2	35.3
..about right	47.7	64.2	50.9	64.3	61.8	62.3	50.6	55.1
..smaller	3.4	3.5	3.7	4.3	4.3	3.2	2.9	3.3
..No answer	6.7	6.1	6.1	8.7	5.2	4.3	3.3	6.3
	100.0	100.0	100.0	100.0	100.0	100.0	100.0	100.0
Balance[2]	38.8	22.8	35.6	18.4	24.4	27.0	40.3	31.9
Technicians								
..larger	7.5	9.6	3.8	3.7	4.5	6.5	11.0	6.8
..about right	66.2	50.8	75.2	67.6	68.4	61.0	51.6	63.8
..smaller	18.6	36.0	13.6	28.5	23.1	29.8	35.3	23.2
..No answer	7.7	3.6	7.4	10.2	4.0	2.7	2.1	6.2
	100.0	100.0	100.0	100.0	100.0	100.0	100.0	100.0
Balance[2]	−11.2	−26.5	−9.7	−14.9	−18.6	−23.3	−24.3	−16.4
Office/Sales staff								
..larger	31.9	17.4	24.6	11.2	16.0	19.6	33.4	23.8
..about right	58.9	74.4	67.6	78.4	75.6	73.7	58.1	67.5
..smaller	4.9	5.6	4.7	5.8	5.9	4.8	6.1	5.2
..No answer	4.3	2.6	3.1	4.6	2.5	1.9	2.4	3.5
	100.0	100.0	100.0	100.0	100.0	100.0	100.0	100.0
Balance[2]	27.1	11.7	19.9	5.5	10.1	14.9	27.3	18.6
Management								
..larger	10.7	10.4	5.2	5.1	5.6	7.4	13.7	8.4
..about right	77.3	74.3	84.9	82.3	82.0	82.5	70.4	78.7
..smaller	7.1	11.8	6.0	6.7	9.4	7.6	13.1	8.5
..No answer	4.9	3.5	3.9	5.9	3.0	2.5	2.8	4.4
	100.0	100.0	100.0	100.0	100.0	100.0	100.0	100.0
Balance[2]	3.5	−1.4	−0.8	−1.6	−3.8	−0.2	0.6	−0.1
TOTAL								
..larger	28.0	19.9	33.3	13.7	19.1	19.9	37.6	27.1
..about right	61.3	57.7	53.7	70.9	65.1	63.7	41.7	56.3
..smaller	5.7	16.9	7.1	9.5	9.9	9.4	14.5	10.7
..No answer	5.0	5.5	5.9	5.9	5.9	7.0	6.2	5.9
	100.0	100.0	100.0	100.0	100.0	100.0	100.0	100.0
Balance[2]	22.3	3.0	26.2	4.2	9.1	10.5	23.1	16.5

[1] Without Denmark, Portugal and Spain.
[2] Difference of the percentage shares 'up' or 'down'.

Source: EC survey on employment and labour market, 1985/86, industry.

Table 40*

Employment trend in manufacturing industry by branch and company size class at Community level[1]

Question: What has been the trend over the last year and what is the expected trend over the next 12 months?

(answers in %)

	Branch			Size class (employees)				All sizes
	Intermediate goods	Investment goods	Consumer goods	Less than 200	200-499	500-1 000	More than 1 000	
Past 12 months								
..up	26,4	43,5	24,4	29,1	38,5	34,7	36,4	32,3
..no change	22,5	23,9	27,3	41,1	25,8	25,4	13,8	24,2
..down	49,4	31,5	47,4	28,8	34,9	38,9	48,8	42,2
..No answer	1,7	1,1	0,9	1,0	0,8	1,0	1,0	1,3
	100,0	100,0	100,0	100,0	100,0	100,0	100,0	100,0
Balance[2]	−23,0	12,1	−22,9	0,2	3,6	−4,3	−12,4	−9,9
Next 12 months								
..up	13,2	31,7	17,3	22,7	22,9	21,2	25,0	21,3
..no change	38,5	39,4	41,2	55,2	46,8	44,2	24,0	39,8
..down	46,1	26,0	39,9	20,3	28,3	31,4	48,5	36,8
..No answer	2,2	2,9	1,6	1,8	2,0	3,2	2,5	2,1
	100,0	100,0	100,0	100,0	100,0	100,0	100,0	100,0
Balance[2]	−32,9	5,7	−22,7	2,5	−5,5	−10,2	−23,6	−15,5

[1] Without Denmark, Portugal and Spain.
[2] Difference of the percentage shares 'up' and 'down'.
Source: EC survey on employment and labour market, 1985/86, industry.

Table 43*

Expected employment effect of proposed changes in manufacturing industry by branch and company size class at Community level[1]

Question: What could be the *net effect* of all the changes described in Table 42 on your *employment plans for the next 12 months?* up/no change/down: if up or down: by what percentage?

(answers in %)

	Branch			Size class (employees)				All sizes
	Intermediate goods	Investment goods	Consumer goods	Less than 200	200-499	500-1 000	More than 1 000	
Net effect next 12 months				Answers in %				
..up	39,3	44,7	47,5	50,0	44,6	38,9	37,8	43,9
..no change	40,5	39,3	39,8	33,3	41,1	46,8	47,5	39,8
..down	11,4	9,7	6,6	10,3	8,6	8,2	5,7	9,2
..No answer	8,8	6,3	6,1	6,4	5,7	6,1	9,0	7,1
	100,0	100,0	100,0	100,0	100,0	100,0	100,0	100,0
Balance[2]	27,9	35,1	40,8	39,7	36,0	30,7	32,1	34,7
				Change in %				
Up by %	6,0	5,4	8,6	8,3	5,6	4,8	4,2	6,8
Down by %	−3,8	−3,1	−3,5	−3,7	−4,0	−3,1	−2,2	−3,6
Overall effect (by %)	1,9	2,1	3,9	3,8	2,1	1,6	1,5	2,7

[1] Without Denmark, Portugal and Spain.
[2] Difference of % shares 'up' and 'down'.
Source: EC survey on employment and labour market, 1985/86, industry.

Table 41*

Obstacles to more employment in manufacturing industry by branch and company size class at Community level[1]

Question: Following is a list of reasons which employers have given for not being able to employ more people. In relation to employment in your firm, could you say whether each reason is very important, important or not (so) important?

(order according to the importance given by companies at Community level)

(answers in %)

	Branch			Size class (employees)				All sizes
	Intermediate goods	Investment goods	Consumer goods	Less than 200	200–499	500–1 000	More than 1 000	
(1) Present and expected levels of demand for your products								
..very important	50.5	44.5	54.1	45.0	51.6	53.8	43.9	49.8
..important	27.1	30.4	26.5	30.7	26.1	24.7	31.5	28.2
..not important	18.5	21.3	14.8	19.4	18.3	18.3	21.5	18.2
..No answer	3.9	3.8	4.6	4.9	4.0	3.2	3.1	3.8
	100.0	100.0	100.0	100.0	100.0	100.0	100.0	100.0
Coefficient[2]	128.1	119.3	134.8	120.6	129.3	132.4	119.3	127.7
(2) Insufficient profit margin due to competition (domestic and foreign), which does not allow sufficient prices[3]								
..very important	36.0	25.8	40.0	34.3	31.9	30.5	32.7	33.3
..important	33.8	29.4	35.8	35.0	32.8	37.3	26.8	32.9
..not important	26.4	40.7	20.7	26.6	31.4	30.0	37.2	30.0
..No answer	3.8	4.2	3.5	4.1	3.9	2.2	3.3	3.8
	100.0	100.0	100.0	100.0	100.0	100.0	100.0	100.0
Coefficient[2]	105.6	81.0	115.9	103.6	96.7	98.3	92.3	99.6
(3) Insufficient profit margin due to non-wage labour cost level (e.g. employers' social security contribution, pay roll taxes, allowances, etc.)								
..very important	35.2	26.7	32.6	39.2	30.4	26.4	23.5	29.8
..important	33.0	37.0	39.8	34.1	38.1	45.4	36.4	34.9
..not important	25.1	30.0	20.5	18.8	24.3	24.0	34.9	28.5
..No answer	6.7	6.3	7.1	7.9	7.2	4.2	5.2	6.8
	100.0	100.0	100.0	100.0	100.0	100.0	100.0	100.0
Coefficient[2]	103.5	90.4	105.0	112.3	98.9	98.3	83.4	94.5
(4) Insufficient flexibility in hiring and shedding labour (i.e. necessary redundancies, dismissals and new recruitment may be difficult and costly)								
..very important	33.2	27.1	38.5	38.4	28.9	28.5	22.4	33.1
..important	21.7	29.9	25.7	22.8	25.7	30.1	36.1	26.3
..not important	38.1	38.3	28.9	31.1	37.7	36.3	37.9	34.2
..No answer	7.0	4.7	6.9	7.7	7.7	5.1	3.6	6.4
	100.0	100.0	100.0	100.0	100.0	100.0	100.0	100.0
Coefficient[2]	88.0	84.2	102.6	99.8	83.5	87.0	81.0	92.5
(5) Rationalization and/or introduction of new technologies								
..very important	32.8	17.1	23.0	19.5	26.1	27.0	26.2	22.7
..important	37.9	40.2	38.1	38.5	40.0	43.3	39.3	38.8
..not important	22.6	37.5	33.0	34.5	28.3	26.3	30.4	32.6
..No answer	6.7	5.2	5.9	7.5	5.6	3.4	4.1	5.9
	100.0	100.0	100.0	100.0	100.0	100.0	100.0	100.0
Coefficient[2]	103.5	74.5	84.1	77.5	92.2	97.3	91.7	84.2

Table 41* *(continued)*

	Branch			Size class (employees)				All sizes
	Intermediate goods	Investment goods	Consumer goods	Less than 200	200-499	500-1 000	More than 1 000	

(6) Insufficient profit margin due to wage and salary levels in your firm

.. very important	11,1	11,6	20,9	17,5	15,8	12,2	9,6	15,3
.. important	41,0	43,6	44,8	43,1	40,6	47,2	44,9	43,3
.. not important	41,9	39,5	27,9	32,4	37,5	36,9	41,1	35,5
.. No answer	6.0	5,3	6,4	7,0	6,1	3,7	4,4	5,9
	100,0	100,0	100,0	100,0	100,0	100,0	100.0	100,0
Coefficient[2]	63,3	66.8	86,6	78.2	72,2	71,6	64,1	73,9

(7) Insufficient profit margin due to other than labour costs (e.g. capital costs etc.)

.. very important	19.5	7,4	26,9	17,5	12,7	11,4	15,3	16,7
.. important	27,1	29,6	31,7	30,9	30,2	37,6	24,3	28,1
.. not important	46,1	55,3	33,4	42,5	47,4	45,1	55,0	47,2
.. No answer	7,3	7,7	8,0	9,1	9,7	5,9	5,4	8,0
	100.0	100,0	100,0	100,0	100,0	100,0	100.0	100,0
Coefficient[2]	66.0	44.5	85,5	65,9	55,6	60.3	54,9	61.5

(8) Shortage of adequately skilled applicants

.. very important	8.6	22.5	12,1	17,4	14,9	14,9	15,8	15.2
.. important	22,8	32,1	28,6	26,3	29,6	26,9	25,9	27,9
.. not important	61,9	42,9	52,6	49,5	49,6	53,9	53,9	51.2
.. No answer	6,7	2,5	6,7	6,8	5,9	4,3	4,4	5,7
	100,0	100,0	100,0	100,0	100,0	100,0	100,0	100,0
Coefficient[2]	40,0	77,1	52,8	61,1	59,5	56,6	57,5	58,4

(9) Increase in contracting out

.. very important	2,0	3,5	3,8	6,6	3,8	2,4	1,9	3,2
.. important	10,6	18,1	12,2	16,1	13,7	16,3	14,9	13,9
.. not important	78,7	71,9	75,8	68,3	72,9	75,0	77,8	75,1
.. No answer	8,7	6,5	8,2	9,0	9,6	6,3	5,4	7,8
	100,0	100,0	100,0	100,0	100,0	100,0	100,0	100,0
Coefficient[2]	14,6	25,0	19,9	29,4	21,3	21,2	18.8	20,3

(10) Insufficient production capacity

.. very important	4,0	3,0	3,2	5,4	4,2	2,3	2,7	3,5
.. important	11,9	10,5	9,6	16,2	15,3	10,4	7,8	10,5
.. not important	75,8	79,4	78,7	69,2	71,3	79,4	84,1	78,1
.. No answer	8.3	7,1	8,5	9,2	9,2	7,9	5,4	7,9
	100,0	100,0	100,0	100,0	100,0	100,0	100,0	100,0
Coefficient[2]	20,0	16,6	16,0	27,0	23.6	15,0	13,2	17,6

[1] Without Denmark, Portugal and Spain.
[2] Coefficient is calculated as twice percentage share 'very important' plus 'important'.
[3] The question on 'Competition' has not been asked in the United Kingdom: the EUR total thus refers here only to 8 member countries.
Source: EC survey on employment and labour market, 1985/86, industry.

Table 42*

Changes in the labour market and their impact on employment plans in manufacturing industry by branch and by company size class at Community level[1]

Question: Looking at the list of possible changes below, which effect do you think each might have on your employment plans for the next 12 months? Significant positive impact/little positive impact/no change/negative impact/no answer
(order according to the importance given by companies at Community level)

(answers in %)

	Branch			Size class (employees)				All sizes
	Intermediate goods	Investment goods	Consumer goods	Less than 200	200–499	500–1 000	More than 1 000	
(1) Shorter periods of notice in case of redundancies dismissals and simpler legal procedures								
.. significant positive	29,0	26,0	37,6	38,4	28,2	26,7	18,3	31,0
.. little positive	23,4	29,7	23,2	25,5	30,1	31,4	24,2	25,7
.. no change	42,5	39,0	31,3	29,8	37,5	38,5	49,9	37,0
.. negative	3,1	3,3	4,9	2,4	1,7	2,3	6,7	3,7
.. No answer	2,0	2,0	3,0	3,9	2,5	1,1	0,9	2,6
	100,0	100,0	100,0	100,0	100,0	100,0	100,0	100,0
Coefficient[2]	78,4	78,5	93,5	100,0	84,9	82,6	54,2	84,1
(2) More frequent use of temporary contracts (fixed-term interim work, etc.)								
.. significant positive	17,5	21,0	23,1	22,4	20,0	16,9	15,8	20,7
.. little positive	27,0	42,1	31,6	30,2	36,8	40,3	44,9	34,4
.. no change	49,4	32,5	33,7	40,5	38,8	39,9	33,8	37,1
.. negative	3,6	1,9	8,3	2,5	1,7	1,0	4,7	5,1
.. No answer	2,5	2,5	3,3	4,4	2,7	1,9	0,8	2,7
	100,0	100,0	100,0	100,0	100,0	100,0	100,0	100,0
Coefficient[2]	58,4	82,1	69,6	72,5	75,1	73,1	71,9	70,8
(3) Better trained job-seekers								
.. significant positive	15,5	21,5	28,1	21,3	16,7	11,0	18,9	22,5
.. little positive	21,8	34,5	23,8	28,7	33,2	33,2	24,9	27,3
.. no change	58,4	40,4	43,5	44,9	45,4	52,7	52,8	46,4
.. negative	2,2	1,5	1,7	1,7	2,1	2,2	1,9	1,7
.. No answer	2,1	2,1	2,9	3,4	2,6	0,9	1,5	2,1
	100,0	100,0	100,0	100,0	100,0	100,0	100,0	100,0
Coefficient[2]	50,6	76,0	78,3	69,6	64,6	53,0	60,8	70,7
(4) Introduction of wider wage differentials according to skills and working conditions								
.. significant positive	19,9	14,4	30,0	30,2	19,4	15,4	10,8	21,5
.. little positive	19,8	32,7	23,3	27,5	29,9	32,0	21,3	25,6
.. no change	55,6	48,6	41,0	36,3	45,6	49,2	64,4	48,1
.. negative	1,8	1,0	1,4	1,3	1,5	1,3	1,7	1,6
.. No answer	2,9	3,3	4,3	4,7	3,6	2,1	1,8	3,2
	100,0	100,0	100,0	100,0	100,0	100,0	100,0	100,0
Coefficient[2]	57,9	60,4	81,8	86,7	67,2	61,5	41,2	67,1

Table 42* (continued)

	Branch			Size class (employees)				All sizes
	Intermediate goods	Investment goods	Consumer goods	Less than 200	200-499	500-1 000	More than 1 000	
(5) Greater emphasis on productivity in determining wages and salaries								
.. significant positive	23,8	16,8	26,1	27,6	20,6	17,2	12,9	21,8
.. little positive	23,1	34,2	29,8	30,2	29,5	33,3	30,3	29,6
.. no change	39,3	39,0	31,6	32,3	35,8	34,4	42,0	36,6
.. negative	10,3	6,8	8,9	5,9	10,3	13,6	11,8	8,6
.. No answer	3,5	3,2	3,6	4,0	3,8	1,5	3,0	3,4
	100,0	100,0	100,0	100,0	100,0	100,0	100,0	100,0
Coefficient²	60,5	60,9	73,2	79,5	60,4	54,1	44,4	64,5
(6) Introduction of 'initial wage rates' (i.e. lower wages/salaries for new starters)								
.. significant positive	18,0	8,6	12,6	25,2	15,8	9,9	4,2	12,0
.. little positive	28,7	34,9	42,5	32,7	34,3	31,5	31,1	36,1
.. no change	49,3	52,6	41,0	36,6	46,0	55,8	61,9	48,0
.. negative	1,6	1,2	0,8	1,8	1,2	0,9	1,2	1,3
.. No answer	2,4	2,7	3,1	3,7	2,7	1,9	1,6	2,6
	100,0	100,0	100,0	100,0	100,0	100,0	100,0	100,0
Coefficient²	63,1	50,9	66,8	81,2	64,6	50,5	38,3	58,7
(7) More flexible working time arrangements at company level								
.. significant positive	12,3	10,4	13,2	18,1	14,4	13,2	9,7	11,7
.. little positive	31,5	37,8	41,0	25,7	29,9	34,1	49,8	38,1
.. no change	49,3	46,8	37,8	47,2	48,3	45,8	35,8	43,8
.. negative	4,1	2,1	4,4	4,8	4,4	4,6	3,1	3,3
.. No answer	2,8	2,9	3,6	4,2	3,0	2,3	1,6	3,1
	100,0	100,0	100,0	100,0	100,0	100,0	100,0	100,0
Coefficient²	52,1	56,4	63,2	57,2	54,2	55,8	66,0	58,1
(8) Reduction of redundancy payments that may have to be paid								
.. significant positive	18,2	17,0	15,0	26,6	18,3	14,3	6,5	16,0
.. little positive	16,9	21,6	35,3	22,4	22,6	22,6	22,5	25,8
.. no change	59,2	55,4	44,8	43,9	54,2	58,5	65,7	52,7
.. negative	3,3	3,3	1,9	3,1	2,5	3,1	3,8	2,9
.. No answer	2,4	2,7	3,0	4,0	2,4	1,5	1,5	2,6
	100,0	100,0	100,0	100,0	100,0	100,0	100,0	100,0
Coefficient²	50,0	52,3	63,6	72,5	56,8	48,1	31,8	54,9
(9) (Higher) temporary employment subsidies for employing unemployed persons, who have particular difficulties in finding a job, (e.g. young people, women, older workers, etc.)								
.. significant positive	12,9	6,6	22,5	18,0	10,7	8,0	6,6	13,7
.. little positive	26,9	28,1	27,2	31,1	32,8	27,9	23,6	27,5
.. no change	56,7	62,0	46,0	45,0	53,1	61,8	67,6	55,3
.. negative	1,1	0,9	1,0	1,7	0,7	0,5	0,7	1,0
.. No answer	2,4	2,4	3,3	4,2	2,7	1,8	1,5	2,5
	100,0	100,0	100,0	100,0	100,0	100,0	100,0	100,0
Coefficient²	51,6	40,3	71,3	65,3	53,5	43,5	36,1	53,9

Table 42* *(continued)*

	Branch			Size class (employees)				All sizes
	Intermediate goods	Investment goods	Consumer goods	Less than 200	200-499	500-1 000	More than 1 000	
(10) Functional improvement of public employment offices (better services provided by official employment agencies regarding job-seekers, professional training, etc.)								
.. significant positive	9,8	7,4	5,4	9,2	7,0	4,0	5,7	7,2
.. little positive	14,7	27,9	29,4	22,8	21,5	23,4	22,4	24,9
.. no change	72,7	61,5	61,2	62,3	68,0	70,4	70,8	64,5
.. negative	0,1	0,1	0,5	1,0	0,2	0,4	0,0	0,2
.. No answer	2,7	3,1	3,5	4,7	3,3	1,8	1,1	3,2
	100,0	100,0	100,0	100,0	100,0	100,0	100,0	100,0
Coefficient[2]	34,1	42,6	39,6	40,1	35,5	31,1	33,8	39,0
(11) Reduction in standard weekly working hours without increasing total production costs (i.e. cost-neutral)								
.. significant positive	8,9	15,7	9,5	10,2	13,8	13,4	13,9	11,5
.. little positive	38,2	30,3	28,6	25,5	33,8	43,1	33,9	31,9
.. no change	36,3	35,0	31,8	35,1	32,7	29,0	37,9	34,2
.. negative	12,7	15,3	26,2	24,4	16,0	12,3	10,8	18,7
.. No answer	3,9	3,7	3,9	4,8	3,7	2,2	3,5	3,7
	100,0	100,0	100,0	100,0	100,0	100,0	100,0	100,0
Coefficient[2]	43,3	46,4	21,5	21,5	45,3	57,5	51,0	36,1
(12) Introduction of (more) profit-oriented components in contractual salaries								
.. significant positive	7,0	9,1	9,3	15,1	11,0	9,1	4,1	8,1
.. little positive	29,7	29,6	22,8	29,2	30,5	30,2	25,1	26,9
.. no change	53,5	52,0	51,4	42,6	46,6	49,1	61,2	52,6
.. negative	7,1	6,3	12,3	8,5	8,3	9,6	7,6	9,0
.. No answer	2,7	3,0	4,2	4,6	3,6	2,0	2,0	3,4
	100,0	100,0	100,0	100,0	100,0	100,0	100,0	100,0
Coefficient[2]	36,6	41,5	29,2	50,8	44,3	38,7	25,8	64,5

[1] Without Denmark, Portugal and Spain.
[2] Coefficient is calculated as difference of weighted positive impact ('significant positive impact' weight +2, 'little positive impact' weight +1) and the negative impact (weight −1).
Source: EC survey on employment and labour market, 1985 86, industry.

Table 44*

Working time arrangements at company level in manufacturing industry — by branch and company size class at Community level[1]

Question: (a) Apart from the length of the standard working week, do you consider that the existing working time arrangements in your company are
fully satisfactory/could be marginally improved/could be significantly improved?

(b) Has your company increased or is it about to increase significantly the flexibility of working time arrangements?
Last 2-3 years/Next 1-2 years

(answers in %)

	Branch			Size class (employees)				All sizes
	Intermediate goods	Investment goods	Consumer goods	Less than 200	200-499	500-1 000	More than 1 000	
(a) Working time arrangements								
.. fully satisfactory	26,8	27,2	24,6	40,4	27,0	25,4	16,0	25,6
.. marginally improved	53,3	53,9	59,6	45,2	53,8	53,8	62,6	56,3
.. significantly improved	17,9	17,9	14,2	12,5	17,0	20,2	21,0	16,2
.. No answer	2,0	1,0	1,6	1,9	2,2	0,6	0,4	1,9
	100,0	100,0	100,0	100,0	100,0	100,0	100,0	100,0
(b) Last 2-3 years								
.. yes, significantly	21,0	19,2	8,9	10,1	12,7	17,5	23,9	15,5
.. yes, slightly	27,4	33,6	39,2	22,9	35,2	33,0	38,8	34,1
.. no	48,4	44,7	48,7	64,1	49,0	45,3	35,2	47,6
.. No answer	3,2	2,5	3,2	2,9	3,1	4,2	2,1	2,8
	100,0	100,0	100,0	100,0	100,0	100,0	100,0	100,0
Next 1-2 years								
.. yes, significantly	20,5	12,0	23,7	10,0	11,1	14,6	18,0	19,0
.. yes, slightly	30,8	36,1	30,4	26,4	32,6	35,6	45,8	32,6
.. no	41,3	37,7	37,9	55,4	45,1	38,7	23,9	38,1
.. No answer	7,4	14,2	8,0	8,2	11,2	11,1	12,3	10,3
	100,0	100,0	100,0	100,0	100,0	100,0	100,0	100,0

[1] Without Denmark, Portugal and Spain.
Source: EC survey on employment and labour market, 1985/86, industry.

Table 45*

Main reasons for and against flexible working time arrangements in manufacturing industry by branch and company size class at Community level[1]

If flexible working time arrangements already introduced or planned

(answers in %)

Main reasons for	Branch			Size class (employees)				All sizes
	Intermediate goods	Investment goods	Consumer goods	Less than 200	200-499	500-1 000	More than 1 000	
(1) to use plant more intensively	56,5	67,5	59,5	58,1	55,3	55,4	75,1	62,5
(2) to compensate for reduction in standard weekly working hours	23,9	50,2	16,6	22,2	30,2	33,7	45,5	31,4
(3) to reflect employees' preferences	21,3	30,8	22,7	23,3	25,2	23,9	34,0	25,0
(4) better adjustment to demand	47,1	46,9	59,3	57,5	43,9	43,1	54,6	51,2
(5) other reasons	5,3	4,7	4,9	2,8	5,3	4,6	6,9	5,0

If no flexible working time arrangements already introduced or planned

(answers in %)

Main reasons against	Branch			Size class (employees)				All sizes
	Intermediate goods	Investment goods	Consumer goods	Less than 200	200-499	500-1 000	More than 1 000	
(1) existing working time arrangements are already flexible enough	28,6	30,1	26,7	33,1	28,5	25,1	22,8	26,6
(2) legal or contractual restrictions	14,0	19,2	20,9	14,7	22,8	26,1	15,8	19,9
(3) technical and/or organizational problems	42,3	39,5	39,9	42,0	43,5	37,7	36,2	39,4
(4) working time preferences of employees	19,6	18,4	19,5	24,0	19,3	19,1	14,0	17,8
(5) induced increase of total cost per unit of output	16,5	18,2	13,9	15,9	13,2	17,7	18,0	16,8
(6) other reasons, please specify	3,1	6,4	2,5	2,0	2,9	5,0	7,6	4,5

Table 46*

Split of full-time jobs into part-time jobs in manufacturing industry by branch and company size class at Community level[1]

Question: It has sometimes been suggested that full-time jobs could be split into part-time jobs as a way of reducing the impact of unemployment. Such suggestions can take the form of two part-time workers instead of one full-time, three part-timers instead of two full-time, job-sharing, etc. Do you think any of the full-time jobs in your firm could be split into part-time jobs without significant economic disadvantages for your firm?
No
Yes: if yes, about what percentage of the full-time jobs in your firm could be split?

(answers in %)

	Branch			Size class (employees)				All sizes
	Intermediate goods	Investment goods	Consumer goods	Less than 200	200–499	500–1 000	More than 1 000	
.. No (% share)	58,3	57,8	62,0	69,6	60,5	48,0	43,2	59,4
.. Yes (% share)	41,7	42,2	38,0	30,4	39,5	52,0	56,8	40,6
.. (a) 1-2 (%)	9,4	11,8	11,2	4,3	6,7	11,9	22,0	11,3
.. (b) 3-4 (%)	15,3	14,5	8,6	8,6	13,0	17,6	16,6	12,6
.. (c) 5-10 (%)	12,1	14,2	12,4	10,5	14,7	13,9	16,3	13,0
.. (d) 11-20 (%)	4,6	4,0	4,6	5,2	3,4	5,6	3,6	4,4
.. (e) More than 20%	2,9	3,0	2,6	2,7	2,5	2,4	3,3	2,9
Average (% of total full-time jobs)	3,2	3,4	2,8	2,7	3,0	3,3	4,0	3,1

[1] Without Denmark, Portugal and Spain.
Source: EC survey on employment and labour market, 1985/86, industry.

Table 47*

Structure of employment in manufacturing industry by branch and company size class at Community level[1]

	Branch			Size class (employees)				All sizes
	Intermediate goods	Investment goods	Consumer goods	Less than 200	200–499	500–1 000	More than 1 000	
% share 1985 (according to survey)								
Full-time	96,3	95,9	92,9	94,8	95,0	95,6	94,7	94,9
Part-time	3,7	4,1	7,1	5,2	5,0	4,4	5,3	5,1
Total	100,0	100,0	100,0	100,0	100,0	100,0	100,0	100,0
Of which on a temporary basis	1,7	2,2	2,8	2,5	2,7	2,3	1,5	2,2
Absolute figures (1985, estimates) (1 000)								
Full-time	6 791	9 007	7 475	9 937	3 944	2 765	6 592	23 238
Part-time	263	384	573	543	208	128	369	1 248
Total	100,0	100,0	100,0	100,0	100,0	100,0	100,0	100,0
Of which on a temporary basis	119	207	225	260	111	65	205	542

[1] Without Denmark, Portugal and Spain.
Source: Estimates of Commission's services (absolute figures);
EC survey on employment and labour market 1985/86 (% share).

THE EUROPEAN FOUNDATION FOR THE IMPROVEMENT OF LIVING AND WORKING CONDITIONS

The changing face of work: researching and debating the issues

Luxembourg: Office for Official Publications of the European Communities

1988 - 152pp. - 210 x 297 mm

EN

ISBN: 92-825-8595-6

Catalogue Number. SY-52-88-590-EN-C

Price (excluding VAT) in Luxembourg:

ECU 10,00   BFR 440,00   IRL 7,70   UKL 6,90   USD 12,20

**Venta y suscripciones · Salg og abonnement · Verkauf und Abonnement · Πωλήσεις και συνδρομές
Sales and subscriptions · Vente et abonnements · Vendita e abbonamenti
Verkoop en abonnementen · Venda e assinaturas**

BELGIQUE/BELGIË

Moniteur belge/Belgisch Staatsblad
Rue de Louvain 40-42/Leuvensestraat 40-42
1000 Bruxelles/1000 Brussel
Tél. 5 12 00 26
CCP/Postrekening 000-2005502-27

Sous-dépôts/Agentschappen:

**Librarie européenne/
Europese Boekhandel**
Rue de la Loi 244/Wetstraat 244
1040 Bruxelles/1040 Brussel

CREDOC
Rue de la Montagne 34/Bergstraat 34
Bte 11/Bus 11
1000 Bruxelles/1000 Brussel

DANMARK

Schultz EF-publikationer
Møntergade 19
1116 København K
Tlf: (01) 14 11 95
Telecopier: (01) 32 75 11

BR DEUTSCHLAND

Bundesanzeiger Verlag
Breite Straße
Postfach 10 80 06
5000 Köln 1
Tel. (02 21) 20 29-0
Fernschreiber: ANZEIGER BONN 8 882 595
Telecopierer: 20 29 278

GREECE

G.C. Eleftheroudakis SA
International Bookstore
4 Nikis Street
105 63 Athens
Tel. 322 22 55
Telex 219410 ELEF

Sub-agent for Northern Greece:

Molho's Bookstore
The Business Bookshop
10 Tsimiski Street
Thessaloniki
Tel. 275271
Telex 412885 LIMO

ESPAÑA

Boletin Oficial del Estado
Trafalgar 27
28010 Madrid
Tel. (91) 446 60 00

Mundi-Prensa Libros, S.A.
Castelló 37
28001 Madrid
Tel. (91) 431 33 99 (Libros)
    431 32 22 (Suscripciones)
    435 36 37 (Dirección)
Télex 49370-MPLI-E

FRANCE

Journal officiel
Service des publications
des Communautés européennes
26, rue Desaix
75727 Paris Cedex 15
Tél. (1) 45 78 61 39

IRELAND

Government Publications Sales Office
Sun Alliance House
Molesworth Street
Dublin 2
Tel. 71 03 09

or by post

**Government Stationery Office
Publications Section**
6th Floor
Bishop Street
Dublin 8
Tel. 78 16 66

ITALIA

Licosa Spa
Via Lamarmora, 45
Casella postale 552
50 121 Firenze
Tel. 57 97 51
Telex 570466 LICOSA I
CCP 343 509

Subagenti:

**Libreria scientifica Lucio de
Biasio — AEIOU**
Via Meravigli, 16
20 123 Milano
Tel. 80 76 79

Herder Editrice e Libreria
P.zza Montecitorio 117/120
00186 ROMA
Tel. 67 94 628-67 95 304

Libreria giuridica
Via 12 Ottobre, 172/R
16 121 Genova
Tel. 59 56 93

GRAND-DUCHÉ DE LUXEMBOURG
et autres pays/and other countries

**Office des publications officielles
des Communautés européennes**
2, rue Mercier
L-2985 Luxembourg
Tél. 49 92 81
Télex PUBOF LU 1324 b
CCP 19190-81
CC bancaire BIL 8-109/6003/200

Abonnements/Subscriptions

Messageries Paul Kraus
11, rue Christophe Plantin
L-2339 Luxembourg
Tél. 49 98 888
Télex 2515
CCP 49242-63

NEDERLAND

Staatsdrukkerij- en uitgeverijbedrijf
Christoffel Plantijnstraat
Postbus 20014
2500 EA 's-Gravenhage
Tel. (070) 78 98 80 (bestellingen)

PORTUGAL

**Imprensa Nacional
Casa de Moeda, E. P.**
Rua D. Francisco Manuel de Melo, 5
1092 Lisboa Codex
Tel. 69 34 14
Telex 15328 INCM

**Distribuidora Livros Bertrand Lda.
Grupo Bertrand, SARL**
Rua das Terras do Vales, 4-A
Apart. 37
2700 Amadora CODEX
Tel. 493 90 50 — 494 87 88
Telex 15798 BERDIS

UNITED KINGDOM

HM Stationery Office
HMSO Publications Centre
51 Nine Elms Lane
London SW8 5DR
Tel. (01) 211 56 56

Sub-agent:

Alan Armstrong & Associates Ltd
72 Park Road
London NW1 4SH
Tel. (01) 723 39 02
Telex 297635 AAALTD G

UNITED STATES OF AMERICA

**European Community Information
Service**
2100 M Street, NW
Suite 707
Washington, DC 20037
Tel. (202) 862 9500

CANADA

Renouf Publishing Co., Ltd
61 Sparks Street
Ottawa
Ontario K1P 5R1
Tel. Toll Free 1 (800) 267 4164
Ottawa Region (613) 238 8985-6
Telex 053-4936

JAPAN

Kinokuniya Company Ltd
17-7 Shinjuku 3-Chome
Shinjuku-ku
Tokyo 160-91
Tel. (03) 354 0131

Journal Department
PO Box 55 Chitose
Tokyo 156
Tel. (03) 439 0124